THE WILD GAME SMOKER AND GRILL COOKBOOK

Sensational Recipes and BBQ Techniques for Mouth-Watering Deer, Elk, Turkey, Pheasant, Duck and More

Kindi Lantz

Ulysses Press

Published by:
Ulysses Press
P.O. Box 3440
Berkeley, CA 94703
www.ulyssespress.com

ISBN: 978-1-61243-870-2
Library of Congress Catalog Number: 2018959338

Printed in the United States by Versa Press
10 9 8 7 6 5 4 3 2 1

Acquisitions editor: Casie Vogel
Managing editor: Claire Chun
Editor: Shayna Keyles
Proofreader: Renee Rutledge
Front cover and interior design: what!design @ whatweb.com
Front cover images: shutterstock.com—charcoal © TMON; BBQ meat © Kevin.McCollum; ribs © Arina P Habich; duck and pheasant icons © Sandra P; rabbit icon © KittyVector; running pronghorn icon © Robert Adrian Hillman; running deer icon © Duda Vasilii; standing elk and boar icons © SunshineVector; quail icon © Dagmara Ponikiewska
Interior images: © Kindi Lantz except shutterstock.com photographs on page 5 charcoal grill © galsand; page 6 gas grill © tab62; page 8 charcoal chimney © VDB Photos; page 9 smoker box © Paul_Brighton, page 24 meatballs © Alexey Borodin

Distributed by Publishers Group West

IMPORTANT NOTE TO READERS: This book is independently authored and published and no sponsorship or endorsement of this book by, and no affiliation with, any trademarked brands or products mentioned or pictured within is claimed or suggested. All trademarks that appear in this book belong to their respective owners and are used here for informational purposes only. The author and publisher encourage readers to patronize the quality brands and products mentioned and pictured in this book. Take special note of the important safety warnings throughout this book, and always use customary precautions for safe food preparation, handling, and storage.

To those who strive to live wildly.

To those who work to keep wild lands free.

And to my wonderfully wild family.

Contents

Foreword . . . . **vii**

INTRODUCTION
Raised Wild **1**

CHAPTER ONE
Getting Started **3**

CHAPTER TWO
Grilling and Smoking Basics **13**

Basic BBQ Rub 15

Perfect Poultry Rub 15

Citrus-Ginger Marinade 16

Sweet Heat Marinade 16

Maple Mud Marinade 17

Cilantro Lime Mayo 17

Thai Chili Oil 18

Habanero Carrot Hot Sauce 18

Rhubarb Jalapeño Sauce 19

Garlicky Aioli 19

Root Beer Barbecue Sauce 20

CHAPTER THREE
Appetizers **21**

Venison Steak and Avocado Tostadas 22

Montana Meatballs 25

Hickory-Smoked Montana Meatballs in
Root Beer Barbecue Sauce 26

Mozzarella-Stuffed Meatballs with
Sun-Dried Tomato Dipping Sauce 27

Fire-Roasted Red Pepper and Venison
Stuffed Mushrooms 29

Grilled Nacho Bites with
Seasoned Antelope 31

Buttermilk Steak Bites with
Cajun Dipping Sauce 32

Wild Boar Salami Bites with Mascarpone
and Raspberry Jam 34

CHAPTER FOUR
Salads and Side Dishes 35

Elk Caesar Salad 36

Smoked Duck Salad with Goat Cheese,
Pecans, and Lemon Maple Vinaigrette 38

Spinach and Strawberry Salad with
Crispy Duck Skin and Goat Cheese 41

Asian Broccoli Salad with Pronghorn
Steak 42

Smoked Duck Fried Rice 45

Wild Smoked Onion Bombs 46

Grilled Steak and Potato Salad with
Gorgonzola 48

Smoky Maple Baked Beans with
Venison 51

CHAPTER FIVE
Venison Steaks 53

The Perfect Venison Steak 54

Compound Butter 57

Lemon Butter Dipper 57

Unsurpassable Blue Cheese Sauce 58

Chimichurri 58

Wild Mushroom and Shallot Sauté 59

Smoked Mediterranean Venison Roulade
with Basil Balsamic Reduction 60

Spinach-Artichoke Stuffed Elk Tenderloin
in Creamy White Wine Sauce 62

Prosciutto and Fontina Stuffed Steak
Rolls with Plum Chutney 65

CHAPTER SIX
Burgers 68

Burger Starter 69

Bacon Wrapped Venison Burgers with
Caramelized Onion and Gorgonzola
Cream Sauce 71

Blueberry and Brie Infused Bear Burgers . . 73

The Sequel to the Hunter Clogger 75

Tomato and Mozzarella Stuffed Bison
Burgers with Basilchurri and Butter
Lettuce Buns 77

Cheesesteak Elk Burgers 79

Venison Jalapeño Popper Burgers 82

Antelope Burger with Crispy Sweet Onions,
Green Pepper Cream Cheese Sauce, and
Portobello Bun 84

Goose Burgers with Fig and Bacon Jam
and Goat Cheese 86

Wild Turkey Burger with Swiss Cheese
and Sun-Dried Tomato Basil Spread 89

Enchilada Elk Burger with Green Chile–
Corn Cake Bun 90

CHAPTER SEVEN
Entrées 93

Coconut Milk–Soaked Bison Satay
with Ginger Peanut Sauce 94

Cherry-Smoked Duck with Huckleberry
Cabernet Sauce 97

Russian-Style Elk Shashlik. 99

Honey-Soy Duck Skewers 100

Hawaiian-Style Boozy Boozy Duck 101

Smoked Cider Braised Quail 103

Hickory-Smoked Maple Rabbit 105

Cherry-Glazed Whole Smoked Pheasant
with Cornbread Stuffing 107

Bison Bulgogi 109

Grilled Bacon-Wrapped Meatloaf Topped
with White Cheddar Mashed Potatoes . . . 110

Spaghetti with Montana Meatball and
Mushroom Skewers 112

Chermoula Spiced Rabbit with
Roasted Pepper Chutney 114

Char-Grilled Venison Tacos with Simple
Mango Salsa and Cilantro Lime Mayo . . . 116

CHAPTER EIGHT
Jerky and Sausage 118

Old-Fashioned Jerky 119

Hickory Honey Jerky. 120

Apple-Smoked Maple and Brown
Sugar Jerky. 120

Sweet and Spicy Jerky. 121

Citrus-Thyme Jerky. 121

Chipotle Mole Jerky 122

Green Chile–Cilantro with Lime Jerky. . . 122

Sesame Soy Jerky 123

Whiskey and Spiced Cider Jerky 123

Bourbon Peach Jerky. 124

Garlic, Cracked Pepper, and
Sea Salt Jerky 124

Black Bear Pemmican with Dried Fruit
and Nuts 125

Elk and Pronghorn Smoked Summer
Sausage. 127

Wild Turkey and Wild Mushroom
Sausage. 129

Hickory-Smoked Venison Breakfast
Sausage Patties 132

Game Meats to Use in Recipes. 133
Acknowledgments 135
About the Author 136

Foreword

At this point in my life, I've been away from Montana longer than I've lived there, but it will always be my home.

On the East Coast, I get this response a lot when I tell people where I'm from: "Wow… I've never met anyone from Montana!" There are a couple of reasons for that… first of all, there aren't that many of us. At last count, just over a million people live in the fourth largest state in the union (only Alaska, Texas, and California are bigger by land area). The second reason is because many of the people who grow up there choose to stay, or find their way back later in life. My cousin (and the author of this book), Kindi Lantz, is one of the latter. As much as I thrive on big-city living, I can't really blame her. There's clean air, miles and miles of wilderness, and a sky that twinkles with billions of stars each night. (As a kid, I just assumed that everyone could see the Milky Way with the naked eye.)

Of course, there were other things about growing up in Montana that I didn't fully appreciate until I moved away. Like the fact that anytime we wanted some sort of beef for dinner (which was quite often), my mom would simply send me out to the garage to grab a package out of our deep freezer. That's because we would buy a half (or sometimes a full) cow from our friends who raise grass-fed cattle. They would butcher and package it all, wrap it in white paper, hand-label its contents, and into our freezer it would go, ready to be made into hamburgers, tacos, stew, or just a good ol' fashioned steak dinner.

Ironically, it wasn't until I moved away and developed a more curious palate that I started sampling (and loving) the other kinds of meats that Montana has to offer. My immediate family was not made up of hunters, so I didn't even taste venison for the first time until I was living in California, where you either need to know someone who hunts or be prepared to pay astronomical prices at the grocery store—and that is in the rare instances that they would carry it at all. This simultaneously coincided with my newfound obsession with food, both in terms of adventurously trying new restaurants and experimenting in my own kitchen. While I still appreciated the simplicity of what I grew up eating, I also craved the creativity of California cuisine… combining ingredients and flavors I would never have dreamed of as a kid.

That's why I love Kindi's take on wild game cooking. Sure, you'll find standard preparations for things like steaks and burgers. But Kindi will show you how to enhance those flavors with things like compound butters or an herb chimichurri sauce. The Appetizers chapter is where this book especially shines, giving fresh takes on game meat preparation, like Grilled Nacho Bites with Seasoned Antelope or Mozzarella-Stuffed Meatballs with Sun-Dried Tomato Dipping Sauce. In the salads and sides chapter, the Smoked Duck Fried Rice definitely caught my eye, and the Cherry-Smoked Duck with Huckleberry Cabernet Sauce from the Entrées section had me salivating. For the more experienced smokers out there, there is also a whole section on making your own jerky and summer sausage. And, if for some reason you ended up with this book but do not care for game meat, most of these recipes would be easily adaptable using beef, pork, or poultry.

I urge you to get outside your comfort zone and try something new from this book! And while I will not be smoking meats anytime soon in my NYC apartment, I will definitely be incorporating some of these ideas into my next rooftop BBQ.

Jaymee Sire
Food blogger, TV host, and Montana girl at heart

Jaymee Sire is a television host, food blogger, and adventurer. You may have seen her in the past anchoring Sports Center *on ESPN or making various appearances on* The Food Network. *You can check out her latest creations and travels on eisforeat.com.*

Raised Wild

I often forget that the way I was raised is not the norm; that Montana, in its vastness, provided me far different experiences than those of people raised in other cities, other states, other countries—experiences I often took for granted until I ventured away from my home state. As a child, I'd get bundled up to withstand the crisp autumn air, climb into the back of the pickup truck alongside our loyal, doofy retrievers, and head out through the fields with my dad on pheasant hunts. We'd typically return with the day's bounty before noon.

The first time I went on one of these trips with my dad, I recall that the feeling of sheer excitement was quickly replaced by disappointment when it was brought to my attention that we couldn't eat the birds right away but would first have to age the meat. When we finally did get to indulge, it was always served the same way: Southern fried pheasant with mashed potatoes and gravy. I never had pheasant any other way until adulthood, when I began to explore different cooking techniques. Don't get me wrong, it was delicious; my mother's Southern roots influenced our menus quite frequently, and my sisters and I never complained unless frozen carrots or canned mushrooms entered the scene.

Pheasant certainly wasn't the only game meat that graced our plates. Like many children of my generation, I am the product of a divorced and remarried family. I'm very lucky to have two fathers—both of whom were hunters, contributed to my love of game meat, and taught me to respect the animals that nourish us as well as the earth on which they roam. If you take nothing more from this book, remember those very important lessons my fathers instilled in me.

Whether with bow or rifle, each fall, these two men would fill our freezers with deer, elk, antelope, and a multitude of upland game birds and waterfowl. And while they loved the sport, they went out to hunt regardless of how many feet of snow they had to trek through or the other conditions of the terrain because the meat they brought home would feed our incredibly large family through the winter (though, perhaps the hunting was just a temporary escape from a house full of daughters)!

Despite the diverse flavor profiles of the various big game animals that graced our table, there never seemed to be much experimentation with recipes, which seems to be the norm for other hunting families, as well. Ground venison (in this book, venison refers to meat from the various types of deer) or pronghorn (often referred to as antelope in the United States, despite the fact that it isn't related to true antelope species) were always used in spaghetti, chili, and tacos—dishes with such strong flavors that the unique taste of the meat was masked. Steaks were often soaked in milk, vinegar, or broth to hide the "gamey taste," or dipped in flour and fried. It was only later in life that I realized the flavor of game meat should be enhanced with quality spices and other fresh ingredients rather than covered up!

"Gaminess" is often used as a negative descriptor of meat—something that should be avoided altogether. But I now see it much differently. The flavor of game should be embraced, and that is exactly what is intended with the recipes in this book.

While all of these recipes revolve around grilled and smoked meats, I should make it clear that I do not consider myself a pit master, a purist obsessed with and excited about a singular craft, devoting endless hours to perfecting that one particular realm of cooking. I enjoy all types of cooking and thrive on combining the unexpected, fusing cultures and blending both traditional and experimental methods. I aim to capture culinary artistry in a misshapen sort of way, to cut a metaphorical, gastronomic path between the realms of classic cookery and avant-garde cuisine. Some of the methods applied in these recipes might actually horrify a true, purist pit master. While I do applaud the dedication and skills of these dedicated outdoor chefs and would encourage you to learn from every true pit master you are lucky enough to encounter, I also urge you to experiment, discover your own methods, make every recipe your own, and aim for culinary artistry as much as you do perfection.

CHAPTER ONE

Getting Started

There are as many ways to smoke and grill wild game as there are varieties of game itself. This book focuses on the most popular grills and smokers, several different techniques, and a wide selection of tools to enhance the quality of the dish and the ways in which it is prepared, each of which has its own merits. Cooking wild game is very much an art form. As with painting and sculpting, the artist should follow basic practices and learn from others, but should also develop their own style.

Hot and Heavy: Grills and Smokers

I love having a variety of grills and smokers. Some might say I'm a bit of a hoarder when it comes to culinary devices—some might be right. I truly believe in a time and a place for all of the various grills and smokers. That said, I employ my electric smoker and charcoal grill for most of my recipes. My reasoning is simple: Unless I'm eating jerky, I want my meat to be moist and tender. Sure, you can achieve that on any grill, but cooking at high heat for a short time on charcoal allows me to maintain a moist, tender center while adding an element of smokiness, and I don't have to give up those burnt ends everyone loves! For smoking, I like the electric smoker because of the airflow (or lack thereof). I can get an intense level of smoke without drying the meat out.

But don't worry—even if you only have bricks, charcoal, and a smoker box, you'll be able to make absolutely every recipe in this book, no sweat (unless you get too close to the coals).

Each recipe in this book was developed using a particular style of grill or smoker. These will be listed as the "Grill/smoker" in each recipe, but they are by no means the only option. Regardless of which device you choose to cook with, the important thing is to keep a watchful eye on your meat and ensure it cooks to the appropriate temperature.

Wood Pellet Grill and Smoker

Wood pellet grills and smokers are essentially electrical barrel units with attached hoppers on the back or side for the pellets. These pellets, which burn more consistently than wood chunks or chips, are composed of compressed sawdust from various types of hardwood.

Wood pellet grills and smokers average about $500 per unit. High-end models can reach upward of $8,000, though $8,000 is certainly not the norm. There are plenty of less expensive units on the market, with some priced under $200. A huge benefit of this equipment is that it can be used as a grill and a smoker, and high temperatures can be reached quickly. This allows you to both sear and develop a nice smoke level on the meat. Burgers are exceptional on a wood pellet grill and smoker, forming a delicious caramelization on the outside of the patty and achieving a rich, smoky flavor without liquid smoke (I find that too much liquid smoke leads to a slightly bitter taste at the back of the mouth).

The combustion fan of this unit operates much like that in a convection oven, enabling a deeper color on the outside of the meat while maintaining a moist center. Additionally, it's easy to arrive at and maintain the exact temperature desired. However, while the fan enables food to cook 25% faster than with stationary heating methods, this speed is a drawback when you want a slow smoke, which is why I don't recommend this grill/cooker for extended periods of smoking.

Many pellet stoves come with a cold smoking unit, while others have an option of purchasing an add-on with cold smoking capabilities. Such additions are well worth the cost if you are a fan of smoked fish and cheeses.

Electric Smoker

All electric smokers are heated by a hot metal rod, much like in an electric stove. The wood chips are placed in a box directly above the heating unit. There is typically a vent around the top of the smoker to manage temperature but overall airflow is very low, which facilitates a smoldering effect on the wood chips.

A basic electric smoker (with three to four racks, a drip pan, digital temperature, auto shut-off, and easy-load wood chip boxes) typically runs about $100 to $500 but larger, more high-tech versions can be purchased for as much as $6,000.

Because of their height, it's possible to remove racks and hang sausages in most of these grills. And due to the low airflow, these units are ideal for slow cooking and producing a very moist piece of meat. Plus, of all the grills and smokers I've had the pleasure of using, the electric is by far the easiest to use. Simply plug it in, add wood chips, and set the temperature.

A drawback: Observing your meat during the cooking process can be challenging if you check too often. Smokers with viewing windows are quickly coated with a layer of creosote, making viewing difficult. Others don't have viewing windows at all, so when you lift the lid to check the cooking progress, it drastically brings down the level of heat and lets all the smoke out. I recommend checking your meat as little as possible. Another drawback is that while the electric smoker does produce an incredibly moist piece of meat, the smoker's moisture and low airflow is not conducive to some of those finer things that true pit masters desire: a healthy sear, a good smoke ring, and burnt ends.

Charcoal Grill/Smoker

Charcoal grill varieties are about as abundant and diverse as toppings for burgers. I've seen DIY versions made with bricks and terra-cotta planters or from large rocks and cob (see page 8 to learn more about cob), and I've seen large, intricate grills with attached rotisseries, multitudinous cooking chambers, and hitches. Big or small, simple or complex, the basic structure of a charcoal grill is the same. They all have a basin for charcoal, a cooking surface (grilling grate), a cover, and support. In the most simplistic, store-bought models, the support is usually in the form of a mounted tripod. The covers will vary as well, but most will have a vent to support airflow. Cooking on charcoal is probably the most economic grilling solution.

A small, three-legged tabletop kettle grill can be purchased for as little as $20, while the taller version of the same grill can typically be found in the realm of $30 to $85. Even a charcoal barrel grill is inexpensive compared to the propane equivalent, starting at around $50. However, large, portable commercial grills (you know, the kind with a hitch for traveling to barbecue contests) start at around $3,000, with most retailing around $5,000, but they can easily reach $20,000 for custom-made, pull-behind grills purposed for barbecue competitions or special events.

I first learned to grill using charcoal, so these grills hold an element of nostalgia for me. There are several other reasons to use a charcoal grill:

- **Flavor.** Charcoal adds a beautiful smokiness. If you want to grill food up quickly and still enjoy a bit of a smoky flavor, charcoal is far superior to a gas grill.

- **Temperature.** The direct flame enables a much higher cooking temperature than either electric or gas grills. This makes for an extremely caramelized outer crust on meats.

- **Price.** Charcoal grills are the most affordable type of grill. They make grilling possible for everyone, regardless of income level.

However, despite all the positives, I have a love/hate relationship with charcoal grills. A charcoal grill, though extremely portable, has one big drawback: charcoal. There are two main types of charcoal: briquettes and lump charcoal.

Briquettes are, by far, the most widely used and easy to find variety of charcoal, but regardless of the type you use, they often have additives. Even though we are talking about natural substances, for the most part, people are still wary of them. When using briquettes, never use the quick-light versions and wait until the coals are completely gray to white in color before putting any food on the grill. This takes much longer, but the theory is that any additives will have burned off by that point.

Lump charcoal can be harder to find, but for some charcoal-grilling diehards, it's absolutely the only way to go. The appeal is in that it's 100 percent wood, which means there are no binders. I typically only cook with lump charcoal when I'm doing a quick sear on a steak because it burns hotter than briquettes, though not nearly as consistently.

Charcoal also doesn't burn cleanly, meaning you are going to have a lot of ash to dispose of. Plus, charcoal takes longer to heat up than natural gas or electric grills and smokers, and maintaining a consistent grilling temperature can be tough; it needs a lot more monitoring than other grill options.

Gas Grill

Probably the most complex of grills, even the most basic gas grills require numerous parts to function properly. Like the charcoal grill, there is a cooking surface, a cover, and support, but that is about where the similarities end.

In its most basic form, a gas grill will contain a grill body attached to some form of support, a burner unit, a gas source, an igniter, a cooking surface (which may contain a grate, a griddle, or both), and a grill cover. Additionally, you might find multiple variations of hoses, valve regulators, and more. Aside from the gas source and the grill cover, or hood, every other component is typically contained in the body of the grill. The fuel source is usually offset from the grill and a hose runs the fuel to the burner. Valve regulators, which are often presented as knobs on the body of the grill, control the amount of gas released or the temperature of the grill. The igniter creates a spark at the burner, where the gas is mixed with oxygen, and voilà—science meets meat.

Most gas grills also contain flame tamers, which capture the heat and distribute it evenly. These are made from a multitude of materials, from ceramic to cast iron and various metals. Chefs often prefer ceramic for a couple of reasons:

1. Ceramic heats up quickly and holds heat evenly.

2. Cast iron has a tendency to rust and corrode if it is not properly cared for. To this, I would point out that there is no reason not to care for your cast iron—just ensure it isn't in prolonged contact with moisture!

There are two types of fuel sources for gas grills: liquid propane and natural gas, or methane. Because the majority of propane tanks are portable, most gas grills run on liquid propane, although some folks do prefer to have large propane tanks installed in-ground for more permanent outdoor kitchen setups. Natural gas, on the other hand, is always run to the grill from an underground line. You'll need to contact a professional to provide access to the natural gas line. While you won't be able to take a natural-gas powered grill to any tailgates, it does have its perks, the main one being that you will never have to haul the tank to the local refill station to ensure you have enough gas to get you through your next outdoor cooking adventure.

Small propane camp grills sell for as little as $50, but full-size grills typically start at around $250 and can cost upward of $4,000. If you are planning on purchasing one, start by making a list of what features you find important in a grill, find the grills that claim to have those features, and read reviews.

Compared to its cousin the charcoal grill, gas grills burn cleaner—this is true for both natural gas and propane. Like an electric grill, gas grills can reach a precise temperature in little time and are capable of holding a steady temperature, whereas charcoal tends to fluctuate. I find charcoal grilling to be a more active "sport," which I enjoy, but that's not for everyone. Natural gas is more of a sure thing. That said, there are many more parts to a natural gas grill and if a part breaks, it can be an expensive fix, depending on which part it is.

Smokehouses

Smokehouses are every smoking enthusiast's dream and are relatively simple to make, so it's surprising more folks don't have them.

They can be purchased as kits, contracted and custom built, or fully DIY, but the basic concept is always the same. There is a chamber that houses the meat and other items being smoked. The smoke is piped in from a fire chamber that is offset from the smokehouse, and there is another pipe, or flue, for ventilation. Most smokehouses contain grates for setting and hooks for hanging meats.

Because most smokehouses are built rather than bought fully assembled, the price range can vary greatly. They can be built from repurposed materials for little to nothing or built using elaborate designs, with the price reflecting the materials used. Materials range from all types of woods and bricks, to metal and cinder blocks, to cement and stones, but some of the most eye-appealing smokers I have seen are built using an ancient building technique to create a material known as cob—a mixture of clay, sand, straw, and water. You've probably seen at least a couple outdoor pizza ovens built with this material but smokers of this style are a little rarer. If you are considering building a smoker, I highly recommend researching this building technique and considering it an option.

Spatially, this variety of smoker is superior to mobile units. It can be used for smoking large cuts of meat and hanging other meats like salami, link sausages, and hams for smoke curing and drying. Because the heat source is located a good distance from the smoker box, it is also capable of smoking at rather low temperatures, or cold smoking.

Just make sure you have checked city ordinances and area fire codes before embarking on your smokehouse building project!

Gear Up: Smoking and Grilling Accessories

Just as any artist would, backyard cooks have a wide assortment of tools and accessories available to enhance their work or make the job more enjoyable. Also, preferences vary as to accessory superiority. Keeping that in mind, here is my shortlist of essential grilling and smoking accessories.

Charcoal chimney. This simple device can be found in the grilling section of most grocery or outdoor stores. The charcoal chimney enables outdoor cooks to get natural briquettes lit without adding lighter fluid. To use it, fill the top portion of the chimney with your charcoal and stuff the bottom portion of the chimney with crumpled newspaper, a portion of the charcoal bag, or any other paper you have lying around. Set the entire chimney on the grill and light the paper with a match or lighter. After about 15 minutes, the coals should be well lit and you can dump them into your grill.

Meat thermometer. Meat thermometers are required to eliminate the question of doubt as to safety zones of meat and precision of maximum tenderness. I have yet to find the perfect thermometer (and I have tried a lot). Until I am introduced to an inventor ready to take on the feat of developing a flawless thermometer, though, I will settle on the two-probe digital version.

Currently, my favorite "thermometer" is, well, me. It's the combination of my eyes, my experience, and my touch. I can press on the center of a steak and tell right away whether it is rare, medium-rare, or dreadfully overcooked (some might call that medium to well done). For those just getting started, I have a trick for steaks. Touch that fleshy area on your palm at the base of your thumb. If your steak feels like that, it's practically raw. Many will refer to this as "blue" steak.

Now, touch the tip of your thumb to the tip of your pointer finger and feel the same spot at the base of your thumb. It should have tightened those muscles slightly, making the area a bit firmer. If your steak feels similar, it has been cooked to rare (the best way to eat a steak, in my opinion). Move the tip of your thumb over to your middle finger, feeling the same spot. That firmness is what you should feel if your steak is cooked to medium-rare and is what is most often recommended in recipes.

Should you or your guests desire your steak to be cooked to medium or well-done, you can continue to move through your fingers while touching that spot on your palm to check doneness. Touching your thumb to the ring finger will give you the firmness of a medium steak and moving on to the pinky will give you the firmness of a well-done steak.

Smoker box. There will be times in your life when you don't have access to a smoker or you simply don't want to get out both the smoker and the grill for a single meal. Still, a low-level amount of smoke flavoring on your meat would certainly be a nice addition. In these instances, I get the smoker box out. It's as simple as it sounds—a small metal box that can be filled with wood chips or pellets. It has openings throughout to let the smoke escape and infuse into whatever is on the grill.

Set the box on the hottest portion of the grill to ensure the chips begin smoking, then close the grill lid. Occasionally check the grill for the smoke level. When the smoker box is emitting a large amount of smoke, it's time to throw the meat on the grill!

Cast-iron cookware. Whether you are cooking on a grill, a stove, or over a campfire, at some point in your culinary adventures, you'll need cast-iron cookware. At the very least, you should have a Dutch oven and a large, flat grill pan. Once you start using cast iron, though, you'll likely find yourself seeking cast-iron muffin tins, waffle irons, teakettles, and every possible size of grill pan and Dutch oven. Not only is cast-iron incredibly versatile, it adds a good amount of iron to your diet via the foods cooked in it, and it literally lasts forever if taken care of well.

Meat-tenderizing mallet. Sometimes you just need a really thin piece of meat, especially when skewering or making a roulade. I prefer using a heavy-duty, two-side meat tenderizer because the grooves really get into the meat fibers and break them down, giving you an extremely tender piece of meat despite being flattened. In a pinch, though, a hammer or rolling pin will get the job done.

Metal skewers. While I don't have anything against bamboo skewers and do tend to use them when I'm entertaining large groups, I prefer a metal skewer. The main reason really comes down to the prep work. I often get to the point of cooking the meal and realize I forgot to soak the skewers. Using metal skewers eliminates this potential setback.

Metal bristle grill brush. No one likes a dirty grill. Once the grill is nice and hot, we always get out the trusty metal bristle grill brush and scrape any char off. Sure, in a bind, you can use a wadded-up piece of aluminum foil, but the metal bristle grill brush makes the process much easier.

Silicone basting brush. Marinades can do wonders for flavoring the inner portion of meat, but if you really want to step it up a notch, that marinade should be periodically brushed onto the outside of the meal you are smoking or grilling. Doing so will improve the color, flavor, and moisture level of the dish. I prefer a silicone basting brush to the basting mop because the mops will shed on occasion or hold onto some of the juices from the previous dish. The silicone basting brush can withstand high heat and is easy to clean.

Branch Out: Varieties of Wood Chips and Pellets

Speaking with a smoked meat enthusiast about the art of smoking is akin to sitting down with a sommelier to discuss wine. You'll learn that each wood variety has its own flavor profiles and complexities brought out by the various types of meats, marinades, and seasonings used in each application. Also like wine lovers, individual smoked meat enthusiasts can provide a variety of descriptions for the same preparation or type of wood. And there will be some people who thoroughly grasp the difference in flavor profiles, while others will undoubtedly proclaim, "I really can't tell much of a difference. They all taste smoky and I like it."

Alderwood. Alderwood chips contribute a very mild and slightly sweet flavor to meats and other ingredients. Because it doesn't produce a big smoke flavor, it is better suited for light meats, especially poultry and seafood.

Applewood. Applewood, which produces a slightly sweet flavor, tends to be a favorite among grilling and smoking aficionados. It is probably best known for its uses with bacons and hams.

Because its intensely fruitful smokiness is extremely strong, it needs to be used with care to avoid bitterness. It is excellent with varying types of poultry, pork, and rabbit, but not ideal for venison.

Cherrywood. Cherrywood is my absolute favorite for smoking meats. It is sweet, earthy, and mild, with a subtle fruit flavor that enhances most meat. Additionally, it adds a beautiful, almost mahogany color to meats. It's perfect for rabbit, poultry, and red meat.

Hickory. Hickory is the most commonly used wood used for smoking. It has a recognizable, almost caramel-like flavor that is strong, slightly sweet, nutty, and incredibly smooth. It's a multipurpose wood chip for everything from meats to veggies to cheese, but should absolutely be avoided when smoking seafood.

Mesquite. Mesquite smoke is quite common in Mexican cooking, where everything from tortillas to chiles are cooked over an open flame fueled by large chunks of mesquite wood. It is also a mainstay in Texas barbecue, especially prevalent in recipes for ribs and brisket. Next to hickory, mesquite is one of the most commonly used wood types for smoking. It has spicy undertones with a strong, earthy smoke flavor. Unlike many of the other wood types described, there is no sweetness. It pairs beautifully with red meat and some poultry, but should be avoided with many light meats, as it tends to overwhelm them.

Game On: Varieties of Wild Game Meat

No matter where you are in the world, the available game meat differs from those found in other areas. In Montana, I have access to whitetail deer, mule deer, Rocky Mountain elk, black bear, pronghorn, pheasant, and much more, but I don't have access to game meats that are popular in other parts of the world, like kangaroo, 'gator, wild boar, or yak. While not impossible, it would have proven extremely difficult to get my hands on and include all possible meats in this book. Still, the recipes for marinades, rubs, steaks, burgers, and jerky are extremely versatile and work well with most game varieties. Just be aware of safe cooking temperatures for the type of meat you have available.

Substitutions in Recipes

Ahh, the great debate. Is venison an overarching term for all game meat; should it only be used to refer to hooved animals such as whitetail deer, elk, moose, and pronghorn (commonly referred to as antelope); or should it only be used to refer to smaller species of the deer family, like whitetail and mule deer? I've always grown up believing that "venison" is not a catchall term, and that culinarily speaking, when venison graces your plate, it will always be the meat of either a whitetail or a muley.

That said, the definition provided by *Webster's Dictionary* is "the edible flesh of a game animal and especially a deer."

So, for the purposes of this book, I'm going to meet somewhere in the middle. While I refuse to refer to all game animals as venison, I will happily agree to refer to all members of the deer family as venison, and here's why: While there are certainly differences in flavor between the various deer species, they can easily be substituted for one another in recipes. So, in instances where you see venison in the ingredients list for a recipe in this book, know that you can utilize your preferred meat, whether that be moose, caribou, elk, whitetail, or any other species of the deer family. In most instances, pronghorn and bear are also reasonable substitutes, though they will not be referred to as venison.

Should you not have game meat available to you, beef is a great substitute for venison, bear, or pronghorn, and domestic versions of various species of poultry and rabbit can often be found in grocery stores. Note that in most instances, the fat content of a domestic animal will be much higher than in its wild counterpart. You may want to omit added oils and fats from recipes containing these animals.

CHAPTER TWO

Grilling and Smoking Basics

Temperatures and Cooking Times

For many of the recipes in this book, you might notice that I don't provide exact cooking times, but ideal internal temperatures instead. While executing the recipes, you may notice that you have to adjust the cook times I've provided. There are several reasons for this.

Each type of grill and smoker has different capabilities regarding heat levels and airflow. Both are factors in determining the time something will take to cook. As an example, what might take 4 hours on an electric box smoker could be done in 2 hours on a small pellet smoker/grill combination. While some folks might have a variety of units at their disposal, others may not, and these recipes were created to work with various grills and smokers.

Altitude can also affect cooking times, and not just for boiling water. For instance, the same exact cut of meat cooked at the same temperature will take more time to cook in Montana than it would in Florida.

Probably the biggest difference between this cookbook and other cookbooks in the grilling and smoking genre is the variety of meats. With game animals, there is no real standard for processing meat. Some folks might take theirs to a butcher and have the meats packaged and processed for them, while others might do it themselves to their own liking. If they do take it to a game butcher, they will likely have various packages to choose from, and those differ from butcher to butcher.

Other factors that could affect the cuts are the weather on the day the animal was harvested and the distance it had to be transferred to the butcher. If it's a warm day and the animal has to be transferred several hours to the butcher, some of the meat might be spoiled. If this is the case, the butcher will save as much of the meat as possible but traditional cuts may be altered or cut down.

And of course, the size of the animal is a factor, as well. Typically, the farther the animal is from the equator, the bigger they will be. A mature whitetail buck in Montana averages about 100 pounds more than a mature whitetail in Florida. Thus, the cuts will be very different, size-wise.

Because of these reasons, I've provided ideal temperatures for the meat to be cooked to rather than cooking times. Here is a handy chart for your reference.

Ideal Internal Temperatures for Wild Game Meats

	125°F-130°F (Rare)	131°F-139°F (Medium-rare)	140°-149°F (Medium)	150°F-159°F (Medium-well)	160°F (Well-done)
Venison	Ideal internal temperature				
Bear			Ideal internal temperature		
Duck		Ideal internal temperature			
Quail					Ideal internal temperature
Pheasant			Ideal internal temperature		
Goose		Ideal internal temperature			
Ground Poultry				Ideal internal temperature	
Rabbit					Ideal internal temperature

The suggested ideal temperatures listed in this chart represent ideal temperatures for taste and texture and are not necessarily what the USDA recommends as food safety best practices. Specifically, the USDA recommends all poultry be cooked to an internal temperature of 165°F to eliminate any chance of foodborne illness. I'm willing to take my chances to eliminate dried-out duck!

Note: Wild game can carry trichinosis. Deep-freezing most game meat for at least 3 weeks kills the parasite, but may not work for bear meat. So cook any bear meat thoroughly—minimally to 140°F for just 1 minute, which kills the parasite, or to the USDA recommendation of 160°F.

Rubs, Marinades, and Sauces

If you are like me and a lot of other grilling and smoking enthusiasts, there are times when you get home and haven't the time to devote to an elaborate meal. But, you need to feed your family, and you would prefer to get outside and enjoy some fresh air while doing so, especially in those precious summer months. So, you forage through the fridge or freezer for an available cut of meat to throw on the grill. In these instances, it's nice to have an easy application. These rubs, marinades, and sauces can be prepared with little fuss and kept on hand for instances such as these.

Chapter 8, which mainly contains jerky recipes, also includes some great marinades that can be repurposed for flavor twists on grilled meats!

BASIC BBQ RUB

Great for everything from venison to poultry, this all-purpose barbecue rub makes grilling and smoking quick and easy. Store in a zip-top bag, a container with tight-fitting lid, or use right away.
• *Yield:* ⅔ cup | *Prep time:* 5 minutes

⅓ cup packed brown sugar

1 tablespoon chili powder

1 tablespoon cumin

1 tablespoon paprika

2 teaspoons onion powder

1 teaspoon smoked salt

1 teaspoon garlic powder

1 teaspoon celery seed

1 teaspoon ground mustard seed

½ teaspoon garlic salt

½ teaspoon cayenne pepper

½ teaspoon ground cinnamon

½ teaspoon ground nutmeg

1. Blend all ingredients together in a small dish.

2. Use it as a dry rub or mix it with a few tablespoons of olive oil. Liberally rub over meats prior to grilling or smoking.

PERFECT POULTRY RUB

As the name suggests, this rub is perfect for poultry, but it's also excellent in other applications like rabbit, gator, and even rattlesnake! Store in a zip-top bag, a container with tight-fitting lid, or use right away. • *Yield:* ½ cup | *Prep time:* 5 minutes

1 tablespoon plus 1 teaspoon ground rosemary

1 tablespoon paprika

1 tablespoon onion powder

2 teaspoons garlic powder

1½ teaspoons ground thyme

1 teaspoon garlic salt

1 teaspoon ground parsley

1 teaspoon lemon pepper seasoning

1 teaspoon ground sage

1. Blend all ingredients together in a small dish.

2. Use it as a dry rub or mix it with a few tablespoons of olive oil. Liberally rub over meats prior to grilling or smoking.

CITRUS-GINGER MARINADE

Use this marinade for any meats, especially poultry, pork, and fish. • *Yield:* 2½ cups | *Prep time:* 5 minutes

1 (12-ounce) can frozen orange juice, thawed

½ cup lemon juice

¼ cup olive oil

1½ tablespoons minced fresh ginger

1 tablespoon fish sauce

1 teaspoon minced fresh garlic

¼ teaspoon red pepper flakes

¼ teaspoon sea salt

¼ teaspoon freshly cracked black pepper

1. Mix all ingredients together in a jar or container with tight-fitting, leak-proof lid. Store in the refrigerator for up to 2 weeks and shake well before using.

2. Marinate meats for 12 to 24 hours prior to grilling or smoking. If using with fish, cut marinating time down to 30 minutes to avoid "cooking" the fish in the citric acid.

SWEET HEAT MARINADE

Use this marinade for any meats. It pairs especially well with poultry, pork, and fish, and Asian or Hawaiian-inspired meals. • *Yield:* 2¾ cups | *Prep time:* 5 minutes

1 (20-ounce) can crushed pineapples in 100% juice

1 tablespoon packed brown sugar

1 teaspoon coconut aminos

1 teaspoon cayenne pepper

1 teaspoon Ceylon cinnamon powder

1 teaspoon onion salt

¾ teaspoon paprika

1. Use a food processor or blender to puree all ingredients. Store in the refrigerator and use within a week.

2. Marinate meats for 12 to 24 hours prior to grilling or smoking. Cook meats quickly over low heat to avoid burning (due to high sugar content). Brush remaining marinade on towards the end of the cooking process to obtain caramelization.

MAPLE MUD MARINADE

Use this marinade for absolutely any meat variety—you can really impress a crowd by smoking a rack of ribs that has soaked in this marinade overnight! • *Yield:* 1 cup | *Prep time:* 5 minutes

¾ cup pure maple syrup

2 tablespoons ketchup

1 tablespoon chili powder

½ teaspoon garlic salt

¾ teaspoon lemon juice

1. Shake all ingredients together in a jar or container with tight-fitting, leak-proof lid. Store in the refrigerator for up to 2 months.

2. Marinate meats for at least 1 hour but preferably 12 to 24 hours prior to grilling or smoking. Due to the high sugar content in this marinade, cook meats quickly or over low heat to avoid burning.

3. Paint on additional marinade near the end of the cooking process to get a caramelized coating.

CILANTRO LIME MAYO

I have a little bit of a mayo problem: I want to put it on just about everything. This particular recipe is perfect for Mexican-inspired dishes that have a little heat. The mayo and lime tone the spice level down, enabling one to experience the flavor of the spice. Serve on tacos, tostadas, nachos, and on any other dish that calls for sour cream. • *Yield:* 1 cup | *Prep time:* 5 minutes

½ cup mayo

¼ cup lime juice

1 teaspoon sea salt

1 teaspoon white pepper

2 tablespoons finely chopped fresh cilantro

In a small bowl, mix all the ingredients together well. Store in a refrigerator or cooler for up to 3 weeks.

THAI CHILI OIL

When I lived in Portland, Oregon, I fell in love with this little hole-in-the-wall Thai restaurant. On each table was a jar of chili oil for patrons to freely add to any dish. The flavor it contributed was an astounding, simple spice with a touch of umami. I wanted to recreate the spectacular oil and satisfy my craving. This oil can be used immediately but the longer it sits, the more the chili will be infused into the oil, and the spicier it will get. • *Yield:* 5 ounces | *Prep time:* 5 minutes

2 ounces toasted sesame oil

2 ounces avocado oil

½ teaspoon Korean chili paste (gochujang)

1 teaspoon garlic powder

2 teaspoons ground Thai chilies

2 teaspoons apple cider vinegar

Mix all ingredients in a 5-ounce jar with a leak-proof lid by shaking vigorously. Store in a cool, dry location for up to 6 months.

HABANERO CARROT HOT SAUCE

Add a sweet and spicy kick to everything from meat skewers to scrambled eggs. • *Yield:* 3 cups | *Prep time:* 5 minutes | *Cook time:* 1 hour

½ cup white wine vinegar

6 ounces tomato paste

2 carrots, peeled and roughly chopped

1 tablespoon Dijon mustard

1 habanero pepper, roasted and peeled

2 tablespoons minced fresh cilantro

1. Using a blender or food processor, puree all ingredients until smooth.

2. Place the mixture in a small saucepan and simmer for 1 hour, uncovered, stirring occasionally.

3. Remove from heat and let cool.

4. Pour the mixture in a jar and cap with a tight-fitting lid, or funnel into a swing-top bottle. Store in the refrigerator for up to 6 months.

Pro Tip: Stir in a teaspoon of liquid smoke to this hot sauce right before bottling it and place it on the table at every backyard gathering.

RHUBARB JALAPEÑO SAUCE

This sauce tastes great when added to grilled tacos, drizzled over smoky meats, or atop a burger.
· **Yield:** 20 ounces | **Prep time:** 5 to 10 minutes | **Cook time:** 1 hour 15 minutes

6 cups water

5 cups chopped rhubarb

1 cup turbinado sugar

5 large jalapeños, chopped, with seeds

2 tablespoons apple cider vinegar

2 teaspoons minced fresh garlic

½ teaspoon ground allspice

½ cup chopped fresh cilantro

1 teaspoon cayenne pepper, or to taste

1. Put the water and rhubarb in a large pot on high heat and bring to a boil.

2. After the water has reached a rolling boil, bring it down to a simmer and add the sugar, jalapeños, vinegar, garlic, and allspice. Simmer for 1 hour.

3. Blend until smooth using an immersion blender or food processor.

4. Add cilantro and cayenne pepper.

5. Store in a swing-top bottle or jar and keep in the refrigerator for up to 6 months.

GARLICKY AIOLI

Use this aioli in place of mayonnaise on sandwiches, burgers, French fries, and more.
· **Yield:** about 5 cups | **Prep time:** 15 minutes

2 egg yolks

½ cup lemon juice

4 tablespoons minced fresh garlic

1 tablespoon Dijon mustard

¾ teaspoon sea salt

¾ teaspoon freshly cracked black pepper

4 cups avocado oil

1. In a large food processor or blender, mix together the egg yolks, lemon juice, garlic, mustard, sea salt, and pepper until thoroughly combined.

2. Leave the food processor or blender running and start slowly dripping in the oil. It is very important to drip the oil very slowly for the first minute or the mixture will not emulsify, meaning it won't get thick and will likely separate. Once it gets noticeably thicker, you can increase to a slow drizzle. The whole process should take approximately 10 minutes.

3. Store in the refrigerator for up to 1 week.

ROOT BEER BARBECUE SAUCE

This barbecue sauce is fantastic when rubbed on ribs during the cooking process because it forms a sticky, caramelized coating. It also complements lighter meats like poultry and rabbit extremely well. It can also be served as a dipping sauce. • *Yield:* 2¾ cups | *Prep time:* 5 to 10 minutes | *Cook time:* 25 minutes

1 tablespoon extra virgin coconut oil

1 teaspoon minced fresh garlic

½ teaspoon minced fresh ginger

2 tablespoons Worcestershire sauce

1 tablespoon lemon juice

¼ teaspoon freshly cracked black pepper

¼ teaspoon ground nutmeg

¼ teaspoon ground cumin

½ teaspoon sea salt

1 tablespoon onion powder

½ teaspoon liquid smoke

¼ teaspoon chili seasoning

1 teaspoon liquid smoke

1 tablespoon apple cider vinegar

1 cup ketchup

12 ounces root beer

1 tablespoon pure maple syrup

cayenne pepper, to taste

1. In a small saucepan, heat the coconut oil over medium heat. Add the garlic and ginger and simmer for approximately 2 minutes, stirring frequently to prevent scorching.

2. Add in the remaining ingredients, excluding the cayenne, and stir well.

3. Turn heat to medium-low, stir frequently, and cook for approximately 20 minutes or until sauce has thickened to desired consistency.

4. Before serving, add cayenne pepper to reach desired spice level.

CHAPTER THREE

Appetizers

VENISON STEAK AND AVOCADO TOSTADAS

Traditional tostadas include everything you could want in a meal—sweetness from the corn tortilla, a bit of a kick from chiles, creaminess and saltiness from cheese, smoothness of avocado, tanginess of lime, a good deal of protein, and a nice crunch. They can contain a wide array of ingredients, prepared to the preference of the individual chef. This recipe was made using fresh kale from my garden and a nice cut of venison. It's a quick, easy meal that's sure to impress as you stray from the typical "barbecue" norm! • *Yield:* 10 tostadas | *Prep time:* 12 minutes | *Cook time:* 6 minutes | *Grill/smoker:* charcoal

¼ teaspoon cumin

¼ teaspoon onion powder

¼ teaspoon sea salt, plus more to taste

¼ teaspoon freshly cracked black pepper, plus more to taste

¼ teaspoon chili powder

1 tablespoon minced fresh garlic

1 teaspoon dried oregano

1 tablespoon avocado oil

1 pound venison sirloin

3 cups baby kale or other fresh greens

2 teaspoons lime juice

1 teaspoon olive oil, plus more for brushing grill

1 avocado

10 tostada shells

Cilantro Lime Mayo (page 17)

½ cup white cheddar, cut into ¼-inch pieces

Rhubarb Jalapeño Sauce (page 19), optional

1. In a small bowl, mix the cumin, onion powder, ¼ teaspoon sea salt, ¼ teaspoon pepper, chili powder, garlic, oregano, and avocado oil, then slather the mixture over the venison, and let rest.

2. In a medium bowl, toss the baby kale in lime juice, olive oil, and a dash of salt and pepper.

3. Slice the avocado in half lengthwise and remove the pit. Use a paring knife to slice the avocado, leaving it inside the skin. When the time comes to serve it, run a spoon alongside the edge to remove the fruit in perfect little slices.

4. Bring the grill up to high heat or heat the charcoal until coals turn a chalky white, and oil the grate liberally.

5. To grill a steak that is rare to medium-rare, place the venison steak on the hottest part of the grill for 1 to 3 minutes per side, or until it has reached an internal temperature of 125°F to 135°F. Remove the steak from the grill and let rest for about 5 minutes before plating.

6. To serve, slice the steak very thin. Slather the Cilantro Lime Mayo over the tostada shells. Place a layer of kale followed by the steak, avocado, cheese, and Rhubarb Jalapeño Sauce, if using.

Pro Tip: Cook the meat to rare and toss it in a bit of lemon or lime juice prior to serving. This will help maintain the texture while the acid in the citrus further "cooks" the meat.

MONTANA MEATBALLS

When I first developed this recipe, I had my sister in mind. She had just recently needed to give up dairy and a lot of her favorite things. I used nutritional yeast in place of cheese, and it was absolutely delicious! If you don't have nutritional yeast, no sweat; it's great with Parmesan, too. Dish it up as an entrée with your favorite sauce over pasta, place in a Crock-Pot, and cover with barbecue sauce for a delightful appetizer, or just pop them like candy. • *Yield:* 30 to 40 meatballs | *Prep time:* 30 minutes | *Cook time:* 25 minutes

3 tablespoons olive oil, divided, plus more as needed

½ large onion, chopped

2 eggs

1 pound ground venison sausage

3 mild Italian sausage links, casings removed

½ cup crushed corn flakes or bread crumbs

2 tablespoons Italian seasoning

1 tablespoon minced fresh garlic

1 tablespoon dried basil

2 tablespoons nutritional yeast (or Parmesan cheese)

1. Sauté onion in 2 tablespoons olive oil in a large cast-iron skillet over medium-high heat for 10 minutes, stirring often.

2. Mix onion with remaining ingredients in a large mixing bowl, using a wooden spoon or your hands. Roll mixture into 1-inch balls.

3. Using the same cast-iron pan as before, sear the meatballs in 1 tablespoon of olive oil on either side, adding more oil as needed.

4. To freeze: place the meatballs atop parchment paper on a sheet pan, ensuring none are touching. Place them in the freezer overnight and then move them to a freezer-safe zip-top bag. Freeze up to 3 months and use as you need them.

5. Bake on 350°F for 20 minutes if frozen or 15 minutes if thawed, or follow the grilling and smoking recipes on the following pages.

HICKORY-SMOKED MONTANA MEATBALLS IN ROOT BEER BARBECUE SAUCE

Meatballs swimming in barbecue sauce are always a big hit at parties, but there is rarely any variation in flavors. The hickory smoke and sassafras flavor of the root beer really make this party food stand out. For finger food, keep the meatballs in the slow cooker and serve alongside one dish of clean party picks and one dish in which to dispose of the picks. Alternatively, set out appetizer plates and forks. Or, serve over sticky rice for an entrée for four. • *Yield:* 15 to 20 meatballs | *Prep time:* 30 minutes | *Cook time:* 1 hour | *Grill/smoker:* electric smoker | *Chips:* hickory

½ recipe uncooked Montana Meatballs (page 25)

1 recipe Root Beer Barbecue Sauce (page 20)

1. Fill the water pan (if your smoker has one) with a couple of inches of water.

2. Place the hickory chips in the smoker and bring heat up to 175°F.

3. Place the meatballs directly on the grate and smoke for 1 hour.

4. Meanwhile, pour the barbecue sauce in a slow cooker and set to high to warm the sauce.

5. Once the meatballs are done, add them to the slow cooker and turn the temperature down to warm.

MOZZARELLA-STUFFED MEATBALLS WITH SUN-DRIED TOMATO DIPPING SAUCE

Meatballs are good. Meatballs oozing with melted cheese are better. These Italian-style meatballs are fantastic served as an entrée alongside a simple pasta or risotto, or as an appetizer. They are an ideal comfort food on a brisk fall day! • *Yield:* 16 to 20 meatballs | *Prep time:* 25 minutes | *Cook time:* 50 minutes | *Grill/smoker:* electric smoker | *Chips:* hickory

For the sun-dried tomato dipping sauce

¾ cup Italian-style sun-dried tomatoes in oil

2 tablespoons minced fresh garlic

1 small shallot, chopped

1 tablespoon olive oil

¼ teaspoon sea salt

¼ teaspoon freshly cracked black pepper

2 teaspoons turbinado sugar

1 (8-ounce) can tomato sauce

½ cup water

For the meatballs

1 pound ground venison, pronghorn, bear, or other red meat

1 egg

1 tablespoon olive oil, plus more for cooking

1 tablespoon minced fresh garlic

¼ cup buckwheat flour

¼ cup rolled oats

1 teaspoon onion powder

¼ teaspoon sea salt

¼ teaspoon freshly cracked black pepper

pinch of crushed red pepper, or to taste

8 ounces small bocconcini or mozzarella string cheese

basil, for garnish

For the dipping sauce

1. In a medium saucepan, sauté the sun-dried tomatoes with the oil, garlic, shallot, olive oil, salt, and pepper over medium heat, stirring frequently.

2. After 8 to 10 minutes, when the shallots are translucent and the sun-dried tomatoes are starting to get a slight char on the outer edges, mix in the sugar, tomato sauce, and water.

3. Transfer the mixture to a blender, food processor, or smoothie maker and pulse until smooth.

For the meatballs

1. Mix the meat, egg, olive oil, minced garlic, flour, oats, onion powder, salt, pepper, and crushed red pepper in a medium bowl.

2. Place the meat mixture into the freezer for 15 minutes. When the mixture is cold but not frozen, it is easier to work with and won't easily stick to your hands.

3. Meanwhile, cut mozzarella into ¾-inch cubes.

4. Begin heating the smoker with about ½ inch of water in the steam pan. Add the hickory chips and bring the heat up to 225°F.

5. Take the meat mixture out of the freezer and, using your hands, form balls with a diameter of 1½ to 2 inches.

6. Using your thumb, make a cavern in the center of each ball, taking extra care not to poke a hole through to the other side. Place a piece of mozzarella in each cavern.

7. Carefully use your fingers to fold the top of the meatball around the mozzarella. Slightly pinch off and smooth the area to close the hole. Roll the meatball just a little more to ensure it is fully closed and beautifully rounded so the mozzarella doesn't ooze out while cooking.

8. Pour a layer of olive oil on the bottom of a cast-iron skillet and heat it over medium heat.

9. Gently place the meatballs in the oil. Cook them for about 2 minutes or until they are starting to brown. Flip them and cook for another 2 minutes.

10. Once the smoker is fully heated, place the meatballs in the smoker and cook for 45 minutes. Pull the meatballs from the smoker and serve immediately or keep them in a warmer or slow cooker on the lowest setting.

11. Serve warm. Pile the meatballs on a plate with the sauce in a small dish off to the side. Adorn the dish with whole pieces of fresh Italian basil or chiffonade about 10 basil leaves to sprinkle over the top.

FIRE-ROASTED RED PEPPER AND VENISON STUFFED MUSHROOMS

Button, portobello, and cremini (baby portobello) mushrooms are such perfect little vessels for stuffing. Their meaty exterior, which takes on other flavors while somehow maintaining their natural fungal earthiness, adds a wonderful depth to any dish. I used to always use cream cheese as a binder but wanted to bring in a lighter cheese to ensure the venison flavor didn't get overshadowed. A mix of ricotta and mozzarella with a bit of lemon was the perfect fit. • *Yield:* 8 to 12 servings | *Prep time:* 20 minutes | *Cook time:* 25 minutes | *Grill/smoker:* charcoal

½ pound ground venison

1 tablespoon olive oil, divided, plus more for grilling

2 large red peppers

1 large egg

¼ teaspoon sea salt

¼ teaspoon freshly cracked black pepper

¾ cup ricotta

¾ cup shredded mozzarella

½ teaspoon dried lavender

1 teaspoon dried oregano

1 teaspoon onion powder

1 teaspoon minced fresh garlic

2 tablespoons lemon juice

2 pounds cremini or white button mushrooms

1 tablespoon balsamic vinegar

chopped parsley or chives, to serve

1. Position your grill grate as close to the heat source as possible. Light your grill. You'll need to get the coals fiery hot or turn the gas grill up to the highest setting to fire roast the red peppers.

2. Brown the venison in a medium skillet over medium heat. This can be done over the stove or with a cast-iron skillet on the grill. When thoroughly cooked, remove from the heat.

3. Brush olive oil on the hottest part of the grill. Place the whole red peppers directly on the grate where you brushed the olive oil. Cook for 8 to 12 minutes. Turn them every 2 to 3 minutes until all sides are charred.

4. Once the bulk of the peppers are charred, pull them from the grill, place them in a bowl, and cover with plastic wrap. The bowl will fill with steam, which will help in removing the skin from the peppers. After about 10 minutes, pull the peppers out and peel the charred skin off.

5. Make a single slice down each pepper and gently pull the stem out. Most of the seeds will come out with the stem. Scrape the remaining seeds out with a spoon. Then, slice the peppers into ¼-inch pieces.

6. Whisk the egg, salt, and pepper in a large bowl.

7. Add the ricotta, mozzarella, lavender, oregano, onion powder, garlic, and lemon juice, and mix until well combined. Once the mixture is smooth, add in the browned venison and roasted red peppers.

8. Remove stems from the mushrooms and fill each cap with the roasted red pepper and venison mixture.

9. Bring grill heat down to about 350°F, brush more olive oil on the grate, and place the mushrooms on the rack farthest from the fire. Close the lid. Cook the mushrooms for approximately 15 minutes or until they are extremely tender and the cheese inside the caps is fully melted.

10. Meanwhile, in a small bowl, mix balsamic vinegar and 1 tablespoon of olive oil and occasionally brush it over the outer portion of the mushrooms to ensure they don't dry out.

11. To serve, top with chopped parsley or chives and offer as an appetizer at your next gathering!

Pro Tip: Mince your mushroom stems and use them to make gravy for a meal later in the week.

GRILLED NACHO BITES WITH SEASONED ANTELOPE

I might be going out on a limb by saying this, but nachos are the best late-night snack in existence. Seriously, is there anything better? A big problem with nachos, though, is that the ingredients are rarely evenly distributed. You might get one cheeseless chip, find that most lack meat or other ingredients, and some chips become soggy under loads of the wetter ingredients. It seems impossible to get the perfect bite. So, I found a solution: individual nacho bites—the perfect bite every time! • *Yield:* 8 to 12 servings | *Prep time:* 15 minutes | *Cook time:* 20 minutes | *Grill/ smoker:* natural gas

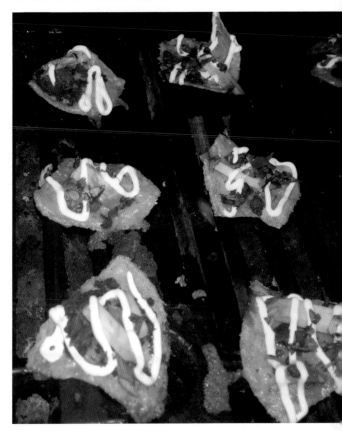

¾ cup sour cream

1 pound ground antelope

2 tablespoons taco seasoning

1 (1-pound) bag tortilla chips

8 ounces sharp cheddar cheese, grated

4 scallions, cut at an angle into ¼-inch pieces

1 large avocado, cut into ¼ x 1-inch-long sticks

½ bunch cilantro, roughly chopped

1. Place the sour cream in a piping bag or into a zip-top bag with a corner cut off.

2. Mix the venison with the taco rub. Brown the meat in a medium skillet over medium heat, either on the stove or with a cast-iron skillet on the grill. When the meat is fully cooked, remove it from the heat.

3. Turn your grill to the lowest setting and lay the tortilla chips side by side directly on the grate, with space between each chip.

4. Put a small spoonful of cheese on each chip. Then add a spoonful of meat, a pinch of green onion, 3 to 4 strips of avocado, and a sprinkle of cilantro.

5. When the cheese has fully melted, squeeze the sour cream in a zig-zag pattern atop each nacho bite.

BUTTERMILK STEAK BITES WITH CAJUN DIPPING SAUCE

These buttermilk steak bites are a tribute to the time I spent exploring New Orleans while I was in college. Though, had I been raised on the bayou, I probably would have replaced the venison with 'gator. Try experimenting with different kinds of wild game; this recipe is perfect for wild poultry, rabbit and, of course, 'gator. • *Yield:* 8 servings | *Prep time:* 8 minutes | *Cook time:* 6 minutes | *Grill/smoker:* no grill preference

For the Cajun dipping sauce

¼ cup mayonnaise

¼ cup buttermilk

1 teaspoon lemon juice

1 teaspoon Cajun seasoning

1 teaspoon paprika

pinch of cayenne pepper

For the buttermilk steak bites

1 pound venison backstrap, cut into 1-inch to 1½-inch pieces

⅔ cup buttermilk

1 teaspoon paprika

½ teaspoon celery seed

½ teaspoon garlic salt

¼ teaspoon onion powder

¼ teaspoon freshly cracked black pepper

¼ teaspoon dried, ground thyme

oil for brushing on grill

For the Cajun dipping sauce

1. In a small bowl, mix all the ingredients thoroughly and refrigerate until use.

For the buttermilk steak bites

1. In a large bowl, mix all ingredients except the steak.

2. Add the steak, thoroughly coating each piece with the buttermilk mixture.

3. Let the steak marinate for at least 1 hour.

4. Heat your grill to about 350°F. If using charcoal, burn the coals to white and wait until you are able to hold your hand an inch or 2 over the grate for about 3 seconds.

5. Brush oil over your grill grate prior to placing the meat on the grill.

6. For rare to medium-rare, place the steak bites on the hottest part of the grill for 1 to 3 minutes per side (for a steak that's about ¾ inch thick). Pull from the grill when the bites reach 125°F to 135°F.

7. Pierce each piece of steak with a party pick and serve on a large platter with the dipping sauce on the side.

WILD BOAR SALAMI BITES WITH MASCARPONE AND RASPBERRY JAM

These salami bites are incredibly decadent. I like to serve them as an impressive appetizer alongside a bold red wine. Dry salami works best, but summer sausage works well, too. If you don't have access to wild boar, use venison, bear, or even wild goose salami! • *Yield:* 30 to 40 bites | *Prep time:* 6 minutes | *Cook time:* 4 minutes | *Grill/smoker:* no grill preference

6 to 8 ounces salami, sliced in ¼-inch rounds

⅓ cup mascarpone

3 tablespoons raspberry jam

6 basil leaves, cut in chiffonade

1. Heat the grill to about 350°F, or until the coals have burned to white.

2. Place a large cast-iron pan or griddle plate on the grill.

3. Using tongs, lay each piece of salami flat in the pan, leaving space between each piece. Grill for about 2 minutes, or until there is a slightly charred ring around the edges. Flip, and do the same on the other side.

4. Remove the salami from the grill and place the pieces directly on a serving plate.

5. To assemble, put ½ teaspoon of mascarpone directly on each slice of salami, and create a slight indentation in the center. Spoon ¼ teaspoon of jam into each indentation then top with a few pieces of basil.

Pro Tip: For a little added flavor, try mixing fresh herbs, honey, or maple syrup in with the mascarpone.

CHAPTER FOUR

Salads and Side Dishes

ELK CAESAR SALAD

I love a good Caesar salad—emphasis on good. Sadly, I've ordered a lot of subpar Caesar salads, with bricks for croutons, watery dressing, and minimal levels of cheese. This particular recipe certainly isn't subpar. It's an incredible combination of cheesy, creamy, crunchy, tangy, and let's not forget the best part—meaty! • *Yield:* 6 servings | *Prep time:* 10 minutes, plus 1 hour to marinate | *Cook time:* 10 minutes | *Grill/smoker:* pellet, natural gas, or charcoal

For the dressing

2 egg yolks

1 tablespoon Dijon mustard

1 tablespoon minced fresh garlic

2 tablespoons anchovy paste

¼ teaspoon sea salt

¼ teaspoon lemon pepper seasoning

½ cup lemon juice

¼ teaspoon seafood seasoning

2 tablespoons white wine vinegar

1 teaspoon fish sauce

1½ cups olive oil

½ cup grated Asiago cheese

For the salad

⅓ cup olive oil

1 teaspoon garlic salt

1 teaspoon onion powder

1 teaspoon freshly cracked black pepper

2 tablespoons sweet preservative-free soy sauce or tamari

3 pounds elk backstrap or preferred cut

3 heads romaine hearts, chopped

4 ounces grated Asiago cheese

1½ cups high-quality croutons

For the dressing

1. Mix the egg yolks, Dijon mustard, garlic, anchovy paste, salt, lemon pepper seasoning, lemon juice, seafood seasoning, white wine vinegar, and fish sauce in a food processor until smooth.

2. With the food processor constantly mixing, slowly drizzle in the olive oil.

3. Once the dressing has emulsified and is thick enough to cake the back of a spoon, add in the cheese and pulse to mix.

4. Reserve ½ cup of the dressing for the salad and refrigerate the rest for up to 7 days.

For the salad

1. Mix the oil, garlic salt, onion powder, cracked pepper, and soy sauce together in a large bowl.

2. Add the elk steaks to the mixture and refrigerate for 1 hour.

3. Bring the grill up to 325°F and cook the steak for approximately 5 minutes on each side or until the steaks have reached desired doneness.

4. Remove the steaks from the grill and let them sit for approximately 5 minutes.

5. Slice the steaks thinly and place them in a large salad bowl with the romaine, Asiago, croutons, and the reserved dressing. Toss the salad and serve.

Pro Tip: Kick your salad up a notch by making your own croutons. Slice fresh bread into bite-sized pieces, toss them in olive oil and your favorite seasonings, and bake on 300°F for 10 minutes. I make a gluten-free crouton using this method and no one can ever tell the difference—in fact, they rave about how scrumptious they are!

SMOKED DUCK SALAD WITH GOAT CHEESE, PECANS, AND LEMON MAPLE VINAIGRETTE

When the idea for this salad occurred to me, I decided it would be perfect to serve to friends we would be camping with at an upcoming bluegrass festival. The crunchy pecans, tangy dried cherries, and creamy goat cheese complement the duck perfectly both texturally and flavor-wise, and the vinaigrette gives it a gentle spike of freshness! For the lettuce, I love a mix of green and red leaf lettuces, baby greens, and/or Bibb lettuce. My friends were astounded by how flavorful the salad was and that, unlike most salads, it was not only satisfying but filled them up, giving them plenty of energy to keep on dancing through the weekend! • *Yield:* 4 servings | *Prep time:* 10 minutes, plus 2 hours to brine and marinate | *Cook time:* 1½ hours | *Grill/smoker:* electric smoker

For the duck

1 duck breast

3 tablespoons pink Himalayan sea salt

3 tablespoons olive oil

2 tablespoons balsamic vinegar

1 tablespoon honey

1 tablespoon dried rosemary powder

1 teaspoon dried sage

¼ teaspoon cardamom

¼ teaspoon freshly cracked black pepper

¼ teaspoon onion powder

¼ teaspoon garlic powder

For the lemon maple vinaigrette

6 sprigs fresh thyme

1 clove fresh garlic

3 tablespoons pure maple syrup

2 tablespoons apple cider vinegar

¼ cup lemon juice

¾ cup extra virgin olive oil

pinch of sea salt

pinch of freshly cracked black pepper

For the salad

10 to 12 ounces of fresh lettuces

½ cup chopped pecans

4 ounces goat cheese

½ cup dried cherries or cranberries

For the duck

1. Rub the duck breast completely with the pink Himalayan sea salt and refrigerate uncovered for 1 hour.

2. Remove the duck breast from the refrigerator and clean off all the salt using cold water. Dab remaining moisture off the bird using paper towels or a shed-free cloth.

3. Whisk the remainder of the ingredients together in a medium bowl to make the marinade.

4. Place the duck breast in the marinade and refrigerate covered for at least 1 hour.

5. Add the smoking chips to the smoker, fill the steam pan with about an inch of water, and bring your unit up to 170°F.

6. Smoke the duck at 170°F for about 1½ hours or until the internal temperature reaches 135°F, for medium-rare. Pull it out and let it rest for 5 minutes before serving. Or, wrap it and put it in the fridge for a later use.

For the lemon maple vinaigrette

1. Chop the fresh thyme and place it in the jar.

2. Using a mortar and pestle, grind your garlic into a paste. Alternatively, you can buy garlic paste in a tube and use 1 teaspoon. Add it to the jar.

3. Add the remaining ingredients to the jar and shake well.

For the salad

1. Place the lettuce in a large bowl.

2. Shake the salad dressing well and toss it with the greens a little at a time, ensuring you don't overdress your salad. Add half of the pecans, crumble and add ¾ of the goat cheese, ¼ cup of the dried cherries, and toss the salad again.

3. Slice the duck thinly against the grain and serve cold or hot.

4. Fan the duck atop the salad and sprinkle with the remainder of the pecans, dried cherries, and crumbled goat cheese.

Pro Tip: If you have leftovers from the Cherry Smoked Duck recipe on page 97, it goes perfectly with this salad, cold or hot! You can also candy your pecans by tossing them in a cast-iron pan with a mix of butter, cinnamon, and brown sugar and cooking them on medium-high heat until the butter begins to bubble around the pecans. Let them cool before chopping.

SPINACH AND STRAWBERRY SALAD WITH CRISPY DUCK SKIN AND GOAT CHEESE

Spinach and strawberries are such a beautiful pairing—both visually and when it comes to taste. The sweet and juicy strawberries are further enhanced by the creaminess of the goat cheese, and the crispy duck skin contributes a surprising crunch that puts the average crouton to shame. • *Yield:* 6 servings | *Prep time:* 10 minutes | *Cook time:* 2 to 3 minutes | *Grill/smoker:* no grill preference

For the dressing

¼ cup extra virgin olive oil

¼ cup red wine vinegar

3 tablespoons lemon juice

2 tablespoons minced fresh thyme

1 tablespoon maple syrup

1 teaspoon dijon mustard

½ teaspoon minced fresh garlic

pinch of freshly cracked black pepper

pinch of sea salt

For the salad

2 tablespoons duck fat or olive oil

8 ounces duck skin, sliced in 1-inch x ½-inch pieces

8 ounces baby spinach leaves

6 ounces sliced strawberries

½ red onion, sliced thinly

½ cup crumbled goat cheese

¼ cup shelled sunflower seeds

For the dressing

1. Add all dressing ingredients together in a leak-proof jar, shaking vigorously to combine.

2. Just prior to tossing the salad, shake the dressing to mix again.

For the salad

1. Heat the grill to about 350°F, or until the coals have burned to white.

2. Place a large cast-iron pan on top of the grill and melt the duck fat.

3. Carefully place the duck skin in the pan. Fry the skin for about 30 seconds per side, until it is crispy and golden brown.

4. Remove the duck skin from the pan and place it on a plate with paper towels to absorb the excess oil.

5. Add the crispy duck skin and all the remaining ingredients to a large salad bowl. Toss with dressing immediately before serving.

ASIAN BROCCOLI SALAD WITH PRONGHORN STEAK

This broccoli salad combines sweetness from oranges, crunchiness from water chestnuts, and tender, melt-in-your mouth smoked pronghorn, and it's rounded out with a pop of traditional Asian flavors. It can be served as a satisfying entrée or a side to any of your other favorite grilled or smoked dishes. • *Yield:* 8 servings | *Prep time:* 10 minutes, plus at least 4 hours to marinate | *Cook time:* 1 hour | *Grill/smoker:* electric or pellet smoker | *Chips:* cherrywood

For the steak

2 tablespoons preservative-free soy sauce or tamari

1 tablespoon chili sesame oil

1 tablespoon pure maple syrup

1 tablespoon white wine vinegar

¼ teaspoon garlic salt

½ teaspoon ginger paste

1 pound pronghorn round steaks

For the dressing

½ cup sesame oil

⅓ cup preservative-free soy sauce or tamari

¼ cup red wine vinegar

⅓ cup mayonnaise

⅓ cup brown sugar

1 tablespoon minced fresh garlic

For the salad

6 cups broccoli florets

8 ounces water chestnuts, chopped into ¼-inch pieces

3 clementines, sections divided and cut into thirds

For the steak

1. Mix the soy sauce, sesame oil, maple syrup, vinegar, garlic salt, and ginger paste in a medium bowl.

2. Add the pronghorn to the soy sauce mixture. Marinate overnight or at least 4 hours.

3. Add the wood chips to the smoker and a half inch of water to the steam pan. Turn the smoker to the highest setting to get a good level of smoke prior to adding the antelope.

4. Place the pronghorn steaks on the grate and close the lid or door immediately to keep in as much smoke as possible. Turn the smoker down to 160°F and smoke the steaks for about an hour, or until the internal temperature has reached 135°F or desired doneness.

5. Remove the pronghorn from the smoker and let sit for 5 minutes. Slice thinly and set aside.

For the dressing

1. Add all dressing ingredients to a jar, cap, and shake until thoroughly mixed.

For the salad

1. Toss the broccoli and steak together in the dressing and thoroughly mix. Let sit for 10 minutes.

2. Add the water chestnuts and clementines to the steak and broccoli right before serving and mix further. Serve cold.

Pro Tip: For a warm broccoli side dish, toss the broccoli in olive oil and roast in an oven at 350°F for about 20 minutes, or until the florets begin to blacken and become slightly crispy. Warm the dressing on the stove, stirring in the water chestnuts and clementines just prior to serving. Toss the steak and broccoli in the mixture, serve, and enjoy!

SMOKED DUCK FRIED RICE

Any time my family smokes a duck, we have leftovers. I repurpose the meat into other dishes such as quesadillas, enchiladas, hunters' pie, and salad. This dish is a favorite, whether as a side or an entrée.

• *Yield:* 8 servings | *Prep time:* 5 minutes | *Cook time:* 20 minutes

olive oil, for sautéing

2 large carrots, cut into ¼-inch pieces

1 teaspoon Chinese five-spice

4 tablespoons liquid aminos, divided

½ teaspoon ginger

¼ teaspoon sea salt

½ teaspoon liquid smoke

1 tablespoon rice vinegar

1 tablespoon orange juice

¼ teaspoon sriracha

4 tablespoons toasted sesame oil, divided

2 cups cooked wild rice

1½ cups smoked duck leftovers

½ cup frozen sweet peas

3 large eggs

3 green onions, thinly sliced, using both green and white portions

soy sauce, sweet chili sauce, or chili oil, to serve

1. Coat the bottom of a large skillet with olive oil and place it on the burner over medium heat.

2. Add the carrots and Chinese five-spice. Sauté until carrots are soft, about 10 minutes.

3. Mix together 2 tablespoons liquid aminos, ginger, salt, liquid smoke, rice vinegar, orange juice, and sriracha, and set aside.

4. Add 2 tablespoons toasted sesame oil to the carrots. Once it is so warm it is glistening, add the wild rice, duck, and peas. Stir every couple of minutes for 3 to 5 minutes.

5. Whisk the eggs and remaining liquid aminos together.

6. Heat remaining sesame oil in a separate pan and add the egg mixture. Using a spatula, lift the eggs up from the pan and fold over. Keep doing this until they are fully cooked. Using the spatula or preferred utensil, chop the eggs into approximately ½-inch bites.

7. Once the rice is slightly crispy on the edges, stir in the sauce mixture followed by the eggs. Top with green onions and serve with soy sauce, sweet chili sauce, or chili oil, as desired.

WILD SMOKED ONION BOMBS

Despite the fact that onions are found in nearly every meal, it's rare that they are the feature of a dish. It's a wonder why. Various techniques for preparing onions produce a multitude of different flavor profiles. When raw, they tend to be spicy; roast or grill them, and they produce an earthy taste; and slow cooking turns them into a sweet, caramelized delight. So, why not make them a vessel and the star of the dish? These onion bombs are great alongside a large, juicy burger. Or, serve them as a comforting entrée alongside mashed potatoes or rice. But don't forget to add a green vegetable to your plate—this dish is extremely rich. • *Yield:* 6 servings | *Prep time:* 15 minutes | *Cook time:* 3 hours | *Grill/smoker:* electric smoker | *Chips:* hickory or mesquite

6 large sweet onions

1½ teaspoons sea salt, divided

1 cup grated Colby Jack cheese

1 tablespoon minced fresh garlic

½ teaspoon freshly cracked black pepper

8 ounces cream cheese

3 tablespoons mayonnaise

2 tablespoons avocado oil

½ green bell pepper, chopped into ½-inch pieces

2 tablespoons Italian seasoning

1 pound ground venison

1. Peel the skin off of the onions and cut off the top ¾ inch (not the root side).

2. Place the onions, root-side down, in a large pot. Fill the pot with water until the onions are fully covered. Add 1 teaspoon of salt to the water and simmer for about 1 hour or until onions are soft but not falling apart. Then, pull the onions from the water and place on a plate to drain and cool with the root-side up.

3. Meanwhile, mix the Colby Jack, minced garlic, ½ teaspoon sea salt, pepper, cream cheese, and mayo in a large mixing bowl.

4. Pour avocado oil in a medium skillet over medium heat. After the oil is hot, add the bell pepper, Italian seasoning, and venison. Cook the venison completely.

5. Pull the venison mixture from the heat and mix thoroughly into the cream cheese mixture.

6. Place the onions in a large cast-iron skillet. Using your (clean) thumbs or the back of a spoon, push the centers of the onions down. You will mash them, making room for the mixture. Take care not to disrupt the integrity of the outer onion or it will fall apart when you stuff it. Fill each onion with the meat and cheese mixture until it is brimming with the stuffing.

7. Bring the smoker up to the highest setting and add hickory or mesquite wood chips.

8. Place the cast-iron skillet with the onions into the smoker and turn the heat down to 165°F. Cook for 2 hours.

Pro Tip: Not an onion fan? The stuffing for this dish is so versatile. Use it to stuff large portobello mushroom caps, bell peppers, or tomatoes for grilling! Or, cook it as is and serve it inside a lettuce wrap.

GRILLED STEAK AND POTATO SALAD WITH GORGONZOLA

My husband and I used to routinely joke about the lack of greens consumed when we would visit our home state, Montana. We used to travel from Oregon back to Big Sky Country for a couple weeks every summer and drive around the state visiting friends and family. Each stop included a backyard barbecue with a combination of steaks, burgers, sausage, and either potato salad or potato/onion foil packs. Occasionally, corn on the cob would round it out, but rarely did anything even resemble a green vegetable. After those trips, we would return home and eat nothing but green salads for days. This is not one of those salads. This is a salad for Montanans—a meat and potato salad. Serve alongside burgers, hot dogs, or other classic grilled dishes at your next gathering. Yukon Golds work best for this recipe, but baby reds can be substituted. • *Yield:* 6 to 8 servings | *Prep time:* 10 minutes | *Cook time:* 15 minutes | *Grill/smoker:* no grill preference

4 to 6 large yellow potatoes, cut into 1-inch pieces

1 (6- to 10-ounce) bison, elk, or other venison steak

⅓ pound high-quality gorgonzola, crumbled

½ cup mayo

½ cup sour cream

3 teaspoons red wine vinegar

½ teaspoon garlic salt

¼ teaspoon freshly cracked black pepper

fresh herbs, to serve

sea salt, to taste

freshly cracked black pepper, to taste

1. Bring a medium pot of water to boil. Add the potatoes and cook until they can be easily pierced with a fork.

2. Strain the potatoes and run cold water over them to bring the cooking process to a halt. Set aside.

3. Generously rub the steak with sea salt and freshly cracked black pepper. Pierce the meat all over with a fork.

4. Bring your grill up to heat (350°F) and brush olive oil on the portion of the grill where you will be placing your meat.

5. Cook the steak for 3 to 5 minutes per side or until the internal temperature has reached about 135°F for medium-rare.

6. Pull the steak from the grill, cover, and let sit for 5 minutes. Cut into small cubes about ¼ inch wide and set aside.

7. Mix the remainder of the ingredients in a large bowl. Once thoroughly combined and no lumps of mayo or sour cream remain, stir in the Gorgonzola with a rubber spatula, to avoid issues with the cheese clumping.

8. Add in the steak and potatoes and stir well. Top with chives, parsley, or other fresh herbs for a pop of color.

Pro Tip: For an extra kick to this salad, drizzle with a bit of aged balsamic vinegar or a balsamic reduction.

SMOKY MAPLE BAKED BEANS WITH VENISON

A grilling and smoking book wouldn't be complete without a solid baked bean recipe. When it comes to baked beans, though, I'm not interested in a dish that resembles bean soup. Baked beans should be hearty, a dish that could be a standalone meal or served as a side to a meaty entrée or among a cadre of potluck items and country cornbread. I incorporate several layers of smokiness in this recipe by smoking the ground venison, adding pre-smoked bacon and liquid smoke, and cooking the beans in the smoker with the lid off. • *Yield:* 10 servings | *Prep time:* 15 minutes | *Cook time:* 8½ hours | *Grill/ smoker:* electric smoker | *Chips:* hickory

2 cups mixed, dried beans, rinsed

6 cups water, plus more as needed

1 pound ground venison

5 slices (approximately 5 ounces) fatty smoked bacon

1 large onion, chopped

2 tablespoons minced fresh garlic

1 tablespoon olive oil

½ tablespoon freshly cracked black pepper

1 tablespoon sea salt, divided

6 ounces tomato paste

1 cup pure maple syrup

¼ teaspoon crushed red pepper

½ teaspoon Hungarian sweet paprika

½ cup spiced apple cider, plus more as needed

6 cups beef broth, plus more as needed

1 tablespoon liquid smoke

1 whole dried bay leaf

1. Place the beans in a large Dutch oven and pour 6 cups of water over them.

2. Bring the water to a boil then turn your burner down to low. Place the lid on the Dutch oven and let the beans simmer for 1 hour.

3. Pour an inch of water in the smoker's drip pan and bring your smoker up to 275°F. Add in hickory wood chips.

4. Remove the beans from the Dutch oven and set them aside. Sprinkle in ½ tablespoon salt and stir.

5. Place the ground venison in the Dutch oven, using a spatula to break it up. Put it in the smoker with the lid off and smoke for 1½ hours.

6. Pull the ground venison from the Dutch oven and set it aside. Add the bacon, onion, garlic, olive oil, black pepper, and remaining ½ tablespoon salt, and place the Dutch oven on a cooktop. Cook over medium-high heat, stirring frequently until the onions are translucent.

7. Add in the tomato paste, maple syrup, crushed red pepper, and Hungarian sweet paprika. Stir until the tomato paste is well blended into the other ingredients.

8. Mix in the spiced apple cider, beef broth, liquid smoke, bay leaf, cooked venison, and beans.

9. Add more chips to the smoker, if necessary. Place the Dutch oven, with the lid off, into the smoker. After 90 minutes, remove the Dutch oven from the smoker and return it to the cooktop. Bring the mixture to a boil, stir, and then reduce the heat to low. Cook with the lid on for 1 hour.

10. Move the beans to the oven and cook at 300°F for about 4 hours. Check the tenderness of the beans and the liquid levels midway through the cooking process. Stir in a half-cup of broth, water, or apple cider if the liquid is mostly absorbed. Stir and scrape the edges and return to the oven for the remainder of the cooking time.

11. Remove the beans from the oven and stir before serving. If all liquid is absorbed, add ½ cup of water or broth.

Pro Tip: Use a mixture of dried beans with various colors and sizes to ensure your smoky baked beans not only astound your guests because of the unique flavors and ingredients but also because of the way it looks. I got the beautiful beans for mine from my friends over at Piece by Piece Farm outside of Olympia, Washington.

CHAPTER FIVE

Venison Steaks

THE PERFECT VENISON STEAK

Less really is more when it comes to the perfect venison steak. Stick to salt, pepper, and perhaps some fresh garlic. This might be the one instance (beyond dating) where too much garlic might actually be a bad thing. And whatever you do, don't overcook it. Venison is incredibly lean and will dry out quickly. It's important to account for both the fat content and the thickness of the cuts of meat when grilling or smoking venison (see Tips for the Perfect Venison Steak on page 56 for detailed information on these factors).

1. Pull thawed steaks out of the refrigerator about 1¼ hours before cooking, and generously rub them with salt and pepper. The flavor of venison is rich and decadent on its own; it should not be overpowered by other seasonings.

2. Once seasoned, return steak to the freezer for about 2 or 3 hours.

For grilling

1. Bring the grill up to 375°F. Use a grill brush to liberally oil the grill.

2. For medium-rare, place the steaks on the hottest part of the grill for about 2 minutes per side or until the internal temperature reaches 130°F.

3. Remove the steak from the grill and tent with foil. Let rest for about 5 minutes before serving.

For smoking

You'll read or hear about a lot of different preparation methods for smoking a steak. When it comes to beef steaks, many grill masters will suggest a dry brine to break down fats and tenderize the meat prior to smoking. Such rules don't apply to venison steaks, mostly due to the fact that there will be very little fat to break down. So, instead of tenderizing the steak, the salt will pull all the juices from the meat and leave you with the equivalent of a meaty hockey puck to smoke.

Smoking venison steaks is something of a science because getting a nice level of smoke is difficult for something that cooks so quickly. Try one of these two methods to ensure a tender, smoky venison steak:

1. You can stick with my original suggestion for a simple preparation of salt, pepper, and a little garlic and then throw your steak in the freezer for 2 hours prior to smoking it. This will allow it more time in the smoker and ensure the smoke flavor has time to infuse the meat without drying it out. Bring the smoker up to high heat before putting your steak in to ensure the chips have started to smoke. Then, turn the temperature down to 160°F and allow the steak to smoke for 1 to 2 hours, or until internal temperature has reached your desired doneness. Refer to the chart on page 14 to help determine the ideal internal temperature for your cut of meat.

2. The second method includes marinating the steak overnight and following the same smoker preparation as listed above. Smoke for 40 minutes to an hour, or until you've achieved your desired doneness. The marinade produces a juicy, flavorful steak, but the levels of smoke will be milder.

TIPS FOR THE PERFECT VENISON STEAK

Cooking venison, pronghorn, bear, and other game steaks is very different from cooking beef steaks. The fat content will be much lower and the protein levels higher. For instance, an elk steak will typically contain about a third less fat than the same cut of meat from a bovine. It's important to keep this in mind when cooking game meats so you don't end up with a tough, dry prized cut of meat.

There are a couple tricks to ensure you get a tender steak every time.

1. The first method is so incredibly simple: don't overcook your meat! I prefer a tender, juicy, rare to medium-rare steak and consider anything with a hotter center to be a culinary atrocity. That said, if you can't stomach pink meat, consider suggestions 2 and 3.

2. Season the steak, let sit overnight, and baste with oil as you cook.

3. Soak the steak in marinade for up 3 days prior to cooking.

As most venison steaks tend to be cut quite thin, getting a nice sear or smoke without overcooking the meat can be quite tricky. A thin cut is fine and dandy if you plan on breading and frying your steaks and drowning them in gravy, but for a decadent, melt-in-your mouth grilled or smoked steak, a thicker cut is better. It gives you a little extra cooking time so you can produce a crispy sear or nice smoke level on the meat without destroying the texture. So, if you take your game to a meat processing center, request ¾-inch to 1-inch steaks, and if you do it yourself, don't stick to the thin-cut standby.

But what about all those wimpy steaks that are already in the freezer? Don't worry, all is not lost. Take them out, let them thaw, season them, and return them to the freezer for 2 or 3 hours before throwing them on the grill. This will allot them a bit more time on the grill or smoker, giving you a nice sear or smoke level on the outside while maintaining a pink or red center.

COMPOUND BUTTER

Compound butters are a great way to gussy up a simple steak. Some of my favorite variations include adding fresh herbs like rosemary and thyme; garlic and cracked pepper; cheeses, especially creamy blue cheese or Brie; and Dijon mustard, with or without fruit or fruit-flavored syrups. I add 1 tablespoon of herbs and spices, but for cheeses, I usually use equal parts butter and cheese. • *Yield:* ¼ pound | *Prep time:* 5 minutes

herbs, spices, and seasoning elements, as desired

¼ pound butter at room temperature

1. Using a blender or food processor, mix your desired ingredients into the butter.

2. Once the butter and desired ingredients have been thoroughly blended, add them to a piping bag to pipe directly onto the steak, or use plastic wrap to shape the compound butter into a typical stick of butter to freeze. Pull from the freezer as needed and slice to don a steak.

LEMON BUTTER DIPPER

The delightful, aromatic blend of citrus and butter enrich the flavor of a well-cooked, juicy steak. The lemon brightens the dish with a tangy, refreshing bite that is balanced with the creamy butter. • *Yield:* ¼ cup | *Prep time:* 5 minutes | *Cook time:* 8 to 10 minutes

1 tablespoon minced fresh garlic

1 tablespoon fresh lemon juice

¼ teaspoon turmeric, optional

¼ teaspoon finely chopped fresh rosemary

½ cup unsalted butter

1 tablespoon heavy whipping cream

sea salt and freshly cracked black pepper, to taste

1. Pulse garlic, lemon juice, turmeric, if using, rosemary, salt, and pepper in a food processor until they form a smooth paste.

2. Melt the butter over medium-high heat in a small saucepan.

3. Mix in the lemon-garlic paste and cream in with the butter and cook on low for another 2 minutes.

4. Return the mixture to the food processor and pulse.

5. To serve, place in a dish and serve as a dipping sauce for your favorite cut of steak or drizzle over the top.

UNSURPASSABLE BLUE CHEESE SAUCE

I'm a sauce person, and I especially love a rich, creamy blue cheese sauce to pair with steaks. The quality of cheese used in this sauce really makes a difference; try to find creamy Roquefort or Stilton. • *Yield:* 1 cup | *Prep time:* 8 minutes

½ cup crumbled or cut blue cheese, divided
2 tablespoons red wine vinegar
¼ cup mayonnaise
¼ cup sour cream
½ teaspoon dried parsley flakes
½ teaspoon minced fresh garlic
¼ teaspoon sea salt
¼ teaspoon freshly cracked black pepper

1. In a blender, blend ¼ cup of blue cheese and red wine vinegar until a paste has formed.

2. Add the mayonnaise, sour cream, dried parsley flakes, garlic, sea salt, and cracked pepper, and further blend until ingredients are well combined. Then, stir in the remaining ¼ cup of blue cheese.

3. To serve, drizzle atop a perfectly cooked, choice-cut steak or serve as a dipper for steak bites or other meaty sauce vessels.

Pro Tip: Make yours a smoky blue cheese sauce by adding a teaspoon of liquid smoke.

CHIMICHURRI

Chimichurri is such a refreshing and unexpected steak enhancement, and the bright green herbs and red flecks of red pepper offer a gorgeous contrast to the deep brown outer edge of a perfectly seared, grilled, or smoked steak. • *Yield:* ¾ cup | *Prep time:* 6 minutes

¼ cup extra virgin olive oil
1 bunch chopped fresh parsley
¼ cup chopped fresh cilantro
1 tablespoon minced fresh oregano
2 tablespoons red wine vinegar
¼ teaspoon crushed red pepper

Mix all the ingredients together well in a small bowl. The oil will separate. Stir again before serving.

Pro Tip: Want a fresh herb concoction to top your steak, but not a fan of cilantro? Make a gremolata by omitting the cilantro and oregano and replacing the vinegar with lemon juice.

WILD MUSHROOM AND SHALLOT SAUTÉ

I'm appalled when I go to a steak house and sautéed mushrooms don't appear on the menu as an optional topping. Any mushrooms are good, but wild mushrooms contribute an earthy and almost buttery flavor to each bite. For this recipe, I suggest using shiitakes or portobellos. Serve these mushrooms atop a perfectly cooked, choice-cut steak. • *Yield:* 4 servings | *Prep time:* 5 minutes | *Cook time:* 11 minutes

2 tablespoons extra-virgin olive oil

2 tablespoons butter, divided

½ pound wild mushrooms, stems removed, sliced ¼ inch thick lengthwise

2 large shallots, thinly sliced

3 large cloves garlic, coarsely chopped

¼ teaspoon freshly cracked black pepper

⅓ cup mushroom broth

truffle salt, for finishing

1. Heat a large cast-iron skillet over medium heat. Add the olive oil and 1 tablespoon of butter.

2. Once the butter is melted, stir in the mushrooms, shallots, garlic, and black pepper. Sauté, stirring frequently to avoid burning but taking care not to overcrowd the mushrooms. Cook until the shallot is translucent and the mushrooms are slightly golden in color, about 8 minutes.

3. Pour in the broth and continue cooking for 3 more minutes.

4. Remove the skillet from the burner. Stir in the remaining tablespoon of butter and the truffle salt.

SMOKED MEDITERRANEAN VENISON ROULADE WITH BASIL BALSAMIC REDUCTION

This flavor combination will jazz up any dish. The sweetness of the tomatoes and basil meld beautifully with the salty kalamata olives, and the tanginess from the feta makes the entire dish pop. It's a wonder why such ingredients aren't used to enhance venison dishes more often. Place the stuffed medallions atop mashed potatoes, creamy polenta, or alongside a simple green salad. Serve warm. • *Yield:* 4 servings | *Prep time:* 15 minutes | *Grill/smoker:* electric smoker | *Chips:* cherrywood

For the reduction
20 to 25 large basil leaves

½ teaspoon minced fresh garlic

1 shallot, coarsely chopped

1½ cups balsamic vinegar

For the stuffed backstrap
½ cup sun-dried tomatoes in olive oil and Italian herbs

¼ cup kalamata olives

½ cup curly parsley, stems removed

1 tablespoon minced fresh garlic

¼ teaspoon sea salt

pinch of freshly cracked black pepper

¾ cup feta crumbles

1 pound venison backstrap medallions

pine nuts, for garnish

For the reduction

1. Add all of the ingredients for the reduction to a small pot and bring to boil.

2. After 10 minutes, lower heat and let simmer until the mixture has reduced to half or until it is thick enough to lightly coat the spoon, approximately 20 minutes, depending on depth of your pot and heat intensity of the stove.

3. Pour reduction through a fine mesh strainer into a small bowl. Discard the shallot, basil, and garlic, and set the sauce aside.

For the backstrap

1. Place the sun-dried tomatoes, olives, parsley, garlic, salt, and pepper in food processor and pulse until all ingredients are minced. Stir in the feta and set the mixture aside.

2. Place the backstrap in a large freezer bag and pound it using a meat-tenderizing mallet until it's about ¼ inch thick.

3. Spread 1 or 2 tablespoons of the olive mixture over each piece of meat, avoiding about a quarter inch around the outer edge. Roll the medallions with care so the mixture doesn't spill out. Tie a 4-inch piece of cooking twine on each end of the roll to prevent it from coming apart in the cooking process. Place on a plate and refrigerate until you are ready to put the medallions in the smoker. Cover if they are going to sit in the refrigerator for longer than an hour.

4. Add wood chips to smoker and heat up to 225°F.

5. Place the venison in smoker and smoke until the internal temperature reaches 130°F, for medium-rare. Remove the venison from the smoker, wrap in foil, and let sit for 5 minutes before serving.

6. Drizzle with balsamic reduction and top with pine nuts.

SPINACH-ARTICHOKE STUFFED ELK TENDERLOIN IN CREAMY WHITE WINE SAUCE

Spinach and artichokes are frequently found together in cheesy dips at events such as Super Bowl parties and potlucks. Occasionally these dips also feature lobster, crab, or even chicken, but I had never seen them paired with steak until I had to come up with a last-minute dish to bring to an event and I incorporated tiny bits of steak into the dip on a whim. It was a hit and led to more recipes using this atypical combination. • *Yield:* 4 servings | *Prep time:* 10 minutes | *Cook time:* 8 minutes | *Grill/smoker:* charcoal or pellet grill

For the tenderloin

1 (7.5-ounce) jar marinated, quartered artichokes, juice reserved

2 cups fresh baby spinach leaves

1 teaspoon minced fresh garlic

¾ teaspoon freshly cracked black pepper, divided

½ teaspoon garlic salt

½ teaspoon oregano

¼ cup cream cheese

¼ cup blue cheese crumbles

¼ teaspoon celery salt

¼ teaspoon ground mustard seed

¼ teaspoon garlic powder

¼ teaspoon onion powder

¼ teaspoon paprika

¼ teaspoon dried crushed basil leaves

4 butterflied elk loin steaks

For the sauce

juice from artichokes

1½ tablespoons butter

½ teaspoon minced fresh garlic

½ cup chopped white onion

1 cup sodium-free chicken broth

1¼ cups dry white wine like Chardonnay or Sauvignon Blanc, divided

½ cup heavy whipping cream

sea salt and freshly cracked black pepper, to taste

fresh herbs or spinach, to serve

For the tenderloin

1. Place the artichokes, baby spinach leaves, minced garlic, 3 tablespoons of juice from the artichoke jar, ½ teaspoon pepper, garlic salt, oregano, cream cheese, and blue cheese in a medium cast-iron pan and cook until spinach is wilted and cheese is melted, about 5 minutes. Reserve the remaining artichoke juice for the sauce.

2. Stir the celery salt, remaining pepper, mustard seed, garlic powder, onion powder, paprika, and basil together in a small sauce dish.

3. Place the steaks side-by-side in a zip-top plastic bag. Using a meat-tenderizing mallet, pound the steaks until they are about ¼-inch thin.

4. Pull the steaks from the bag and rub the dry mixture all over them.

5. Divide the spinach-artichoke mixture evenly among the steaks, spreading it on ½ of each steak. Fold the steak over where it is butterflied.

6. Bring the grill up to 325°F and rub oil on the grate where the steaks will be placed.

7. Gently place the steaks on the highest rack of the grill. For rare to medium-rare, cook for 3 to 4 minutes and flip to cook for an additional 3 to 4 minutes, or cook to desired doneness.

8. Pull from the grill when the temperature of the meat has reached 130°F, cover, and let sit for 3 to 5 minutes before plating.

For the sauce

1. Place the cast-iron pan you used for the spinach-artichoke mixture over medium heat. Once hot, the bits of cheese and veggies on the bottom of the pan will start to turn brown and stick (called fond). At this point, add the remaining juice from the artichokes, using a whisk to bring the fond up from the pan.

2. Add the butter, garlic, and onion, and cook until the onion is beginning to brown and the sauce has almost completely reduced.

3. Add the chicken broth and 1 cup of the wine, and turn heat to medium. Stir occasionally until broth has reduced by ¼ and sticks to the back of the spoon when lifted out.

4. Add remaining wine and cream, and turn heat down to low. Add salt and black pepper to taste.

5. To serve, drizzle a good amount of the white wine cream sauce across the bottom of the plate. Place the steak atop the drizzled sauce and top with a fresh spinach chiffonade or parsley. Serve extra sauce on the side.

PROSCIUTTO AND FONTINA STUFFED STEAK ROLLS WITH PLUM CHUTNEY

If there are two things I could never (EVER) get enough of, they're quality cheeses and cured meats. Salty prosciutto and creamy fontina both just seem to melt in my mouth, and they pair beautifully together—especially when you round them out with fruit chutney. This dish is reminiscent of a high-end meat and cheese platter one might find at an upscale holiday party. Serve it with a glass of Pinot Noir and feel free to pat yourself on the back as your guests' eyes roll back in their heads with each bite! (I recommend using Pinot Noir in the recipe, as well.) Serve alongside a mixed green salad, wild rice, or any roasted vegetables. • *Yield:* 4 servings | *Prep time:* 15 minutes | *Cook time:* 42 minutes | *Grill/smoker:* charcoal and smoker box | *Chips:* cherrywood

For the chutney

2 tablespoons cold-pressed, extra virgin coconut oil

1 shallot, roughly chopped

2 tablespoons water

¼ cup light-bodied red wine

2 tablespoons balsamic vinegar

2 large plums, skins removed, chopped

1 tablespoon minced fresh ginger

1 teaspoon Ceylon cinnamon powder

1 teaspoon ground cardamom

¼ teaspoon ground nutmeg

pinch crushed red pepper

2 tablespoons pure maple syrup

For the steak

4 sirloin tip deer or elk steaks

4 pieces thin-sliced prosciutto

5 ounces fontina cheese

chopped fresh parsley, to serve

sea salt and freshly cracked black pepper, to taste

For the chutney

1. Melt the coconut oil over medium-high heat in a medium-sized saucepan.

2. Add the shallot to the coconut oil and sauté for 3 minutes.

3. Reduce to a simmer, stir in 2 tablespoons of water, and cook for about 20 minutes, stirring occasionally, until the shallots have caramelized.

4. Add in the red wine, balsamic vinegar, plums, ginger, cinnamon, cardamom, nutmeg, and crushed red pepper. Turn the heat to medium-low and cook for about 10 minutes, or until the liquid has reduced by half.

5. Stir in the maple syrup and keep the mixture warm to serve over the steak rolls.

For the steak

1. Place the steaks in a zip-top bag so they are alongside one another and not stacked. Press as much of the air out of the bag as you can before sealing.

2. Using a meat-tenderizing mallet, pound the steaks to about ¼ inch thickness so they can be easily rolled. Pull them out of the bag and generously apply salt and pepper to both sides.

3. Lay the steaks out on a plate with 2 pieces of cooking twine laid underneath and about 1 inch from the ends of each steak.

4. Place a piece of prosciutto across the entire length of each steak.

5. Grate the cheese over the steaks, ensuring each piece is liberally covered.

6. Roll each steak, pushing the cheese in as you go. Tie the steaks up on each end with the cooking twine.

7. Light your charcoal. Add the cherrywood chips to the smoker box and place the box on the hottest part of the grill. Get the coals going and burn them until they are white (or, if using a gas or electric grill, heat the grill to 450°F).

8. Place the steaks on the grill with the tie side up and cook for 6 minutes. Flip and cook for another 6 minutes on the other side.

9. To serve, remove the cooking twine and top each steak with the warm chutney and fresh parsley.

CHAPTER SIX

Burgers

BURGER STARTER

Everyone needs a basic, go-to burger recipe that can be used as a standby and can also be enhanced for a more impressive burger. Now you have one! Experiment with your favorite ingredients or just use the recipe for a simple burger with lettuce, tomato, and onion—the sky's the limit when it comes to flavor combinations (see the next several pages of burger recipes for proof). This recipe makes quarter-pound burgers, but c'mon, you know you want more burger in your burger than that!

• *Yield:* 8 (¼-pound) burgers | *Prep time:* 7 minutes

2 pounds ground meat

1 large egg

1 tablespoon minced fresh garlic

1 tablespoon Worcestershire sauce

½ teaspoon freshly cracked black pepper

½ teaspoon ground mustard seed

1 teaspoon onion powder

½ teaspoon fine grain sea salt

2 tablespoons melted butter, bacon grease, duck fat, olive oil, or other fat

Mix all ingredients together in a large bowl until well combined and form into patties of desired size. Use the patties immediately or make extra for freezing and using later.

Pro Tip: You can freeze this burger starter to use it in a pinch. To freeze, place parchment paper on a sheet pan. Situate the burgers on the parchment paper, ensuring they are not touching. Put the entire sheet pan in the freezer overnight. Pull the burgers out of the freezer, stack them with a piece of parchment paper between each patty, and put the entire stack in a plastic bag. Return to freezer and pull them as needed.

BACON WRAPPED VENISON BURGERS WITH CARAMELIZED ONION AND GORGONZOLA CREAM SAUCE

Gorgonzola is one of my favorite varieties of blue cheese. It's soft yet crumbly and has a somewhat sharp and nutty flavor that enlivens red meat. It's an exceptional choice for cream sauces with a little finishing "bite." With a crispy bacon shell hiding a juicy burger patty and loads of caramelized onions, the layers of complexity will astound all those who eat this burger. • *Yield:* 8 (¼-pound) burgers | *Prep time:* 8 minutes | *Cook time:* 20 to 30 minutes | *Grill/smoker:* charcoal

For the sauce

2 tablespoons unsalted butter

2 tablespoons minced fresh garlic

½ teaspoon sea salt

½ teaspoon freshly cracked black pepper

2 teaspoons dried parsley

1½ cups heavy whipping cream

1½ cups crumbled Gorgonzola

2 tablespoons balsamic vinegar

For the onions

3 large onions, cut into ¼-inch-thick slices

½ teaspoon sea salt

2 tablespoon extra virgin olive oil

4 tablespoons butter

4 tablespoons water

For the burgers

1 recipe Burger Starter (page 69), divided into 8 patties

24 slices bacon

8 buns

lettuce, tomato, onion, avocado, and other toppers, to serve, optional

ketchup, mustard, and mayonnaise or Garlicky Aioli (page 19), to serve, optional

For the sauce

1. Melt butter in a small saucepan. Add garlic and sauté on medium-high heat.

2. Once the garlic is soft, turn the heat to low. Add the salt, pepper, parsley, and cream.

3. Once the cream is warm, slowly add in the Gorgonzola and stir till melted. Pull from heat and stir in balsamic vinegar.

For the onions

1. Toss the onions in salt and add them to a cast-iron skillet along with the remaining ingredients.

2. Sauté on high until the onions are translucent and then turn the temperature down to low.

3. Stirring occasionally, cook the onions until they are medium to dark brown, 20 to 30 minutes. If all the liquid cooks off, add a few more tablespoons of water and cook more, until caramelized.

For the burgers

1. Preheat the grill to 325°F.

2. Divide the onions evenly among the patties and place on top, patting down.

3. Put 3 slices of bacon on a plate in a crisscross pattern. Place 1 burger patty onion-side down on top of the bacon, then fold the bacon around the entire burger. Repeat for each burger.

4. Cook the burgers until the bacon is just crispy, on the bottom and then flip. When the bacon is crispy on both sides, the burgers are done.

5. Right before you pull the burgers from the grill, cut the buns in half and place them face down on the grill.

6. Place a burger on top of each bun, smother in the Gorgonzola cream sauce, and serve with your favorite burger toppings.

Pro Tip: Repurpose the Gorgonzola cream sauce for other recipes. It's great over blanched asparagus, as a dip for grilled bread, or atop a thick, juicy steak.

BLUEBERRY AND BRIE INFUSED BEAR BURGERS

These burgers are big—I mean, REALLY big. And they should be. They are made with bear meat, after all! Each contains half a pound of meat and, when you include the cheese, berries, egg, and other ingredients, they are nearly ¾-pound patties! Each bite is an explosion of creamy, meaty, fruity bliss, so despite the size of the burger, you likely won't be able to put it down. You just might need to hibernate after, though. • *Yield:* 4 (¾-pound) burgers | *Prep time:* 10 minutes | *Cook time:* 20 minutes | *Grill/smoker:* charcoal

2 pounds 50/50 mixed ground bear and pork

1 egg

1 tablespoon Dijon mustard, plus more to serve

1 tablespoon coconut aminos

¼ teaspoon allspice

¼ teaspoon sage

¼ teaspoon freshly cracked black pepper

½ teaspoon garlic salt

1 teaspoon dried basil flakes

½ teaspoon onion powder

2 tablespoons coconut flour

6 ounces soft, triple cream Brie cheese, frozen and cut into ¼-inch pieces

¾ cup frozen blueberries

oil, for grilling

4 large hamburger buns

mayonnaise or Garlicky Aioli (page 19), to serve

lettuce and onion, to serve

1. In a large bowl, mix the ground meat, egg, 1 tablespoon Dijon mustard, coconut aminos, allspice, sage, black pepper, garlic salt, basil, onion powder, and coconut flour well.

2. Incorporate the Brie and blueberries evenly throughout the meat mixture.

3. Divide the mixture in quarters and form burgers.

4. Preheat the grill to 375°F or heat coals until they burn white.

5. Blueberries have a high sugar content and tend to stick to the grill. Oil the grate well prior to putting the burgers on.

6. Cook the burgers for about 10 minutes each side or until the internal temperature reaches at least 140°F.

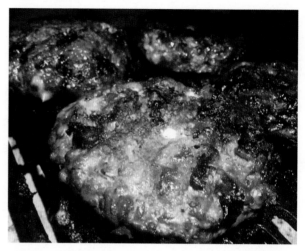

7. Prior to pulling the burgers from the grill, cut the buns in half and place them face down on the grill for about 2 minutes.

8. To serve, slather both buns with mayonnaise or Garlicky Aioli. Place a burger on top of the bottom bun. Follow with Dijon mustard, lettuce, onion, and the top bun.

Note: Various types of wild game carry trichinosis. While deep-freezing most game meat for at least 3 weeks kills the parasite, it tends to continue to thrive in bear meat. Because of this, it's best to cook the meat thoroughly. The USDA recommends cooking meat to a temperature of 160°F, although the parasite will die after the center has reached 140°F for just 1 minute.

THE SEQUEL TO THE HUNTER CLOGGER

My friend Jere, who was working his way to becoming a true pit master—constantly developing new recipes and building elaborate smokers—is the real creator of the Hunter Clogger. Jere conceptualized a burger with so many protein-rich culinary delights piled on top that it would be difficult to fit in the mouth of the average person. Hunter, Jere's roommate, was the test subject for this burger and upon devouring it, he encountered a condition we deemed the "meat sweats." Now, a true Hunter Clogger does not contain the avocado and balsamic onions to balance out its artery-clogging capabilities. Those items are actually replaced with a fried egg and an additional burger patty, but this isn't a true Hunter Clogger—this is the sequel. • *Yield:* 4 (¼-pound) burgers | *Prep time:* 10 minutes | *Cook time:* 15 minutes | *Grill/smoker:* charcoal and smoker box | *Chips:* hickory or mesquite

For the balsamic onions

3 large white onions, cut into ¼-inch-thick slices

1 teaspoon sea salt

¼ cup olive oil

¼ cup water

2 tablespoons butter

1½ tablespoons balsamic vinegar

For the burgers

4 slices bacon

½ recipe Burger Starter (page 69), preferably using elk, divided into 4 patties

2 bratwursts

4 buns

8 slices of cheddar

ketchup, mustard, and mayonnaise or Garlicky Aioli (page 19), to serve

lettuce, tomato, avocado, and other toppers, to serve

For the balsamic onions

1. Place the onions in a large, cast-iron pan and sprinkle with salt. Turn the heat up to medium-low and add oil and water. Sweat the onions until they are iridescent in appearance.

2. Stir in the balsamic vinegar and butter and cook for another 10 minutes, then set aside.

For the burgers

1. Cook the bacon until crispy, cut each strip in half, and set aside.

2. Fill your smoker box with your preferred wood chips and place in the grill. Bring the grill up to 375°F.

3. Place the bratwursts and burgers on the grill with the bratwursts on the hottest part of the grill and the burgers on the top rack or outer edges. Flip the burgers after about 5 minutes.

4. Once the bratwursts are cooked through, remove them from the grill and slice them in half, horizontally. Then slice them in half again lengthwise.

5. When the burgers have reached rare to medium-rare, pile a hefty amount of balsamic onions on the patty, followed by 2 bratwurst slices, 1 slice of cheese, 2 half-slices of bacon, and top with an additional slice of cheese.

6. Place the buns face down on the grill.

7. Once the cheese has melted, pull the burgers from the grill.

8. Slather your favorite burger sauces (I prefer mayo and ketchup) on the bottom bun, place the burger atop the bun, and then add the tomato, avocado, and lettuce. Serve alongside a refreshing salad to balance the excessive, meaty goodness and prevent the "meat sweats."

TOMATO AND MOZZARELLA STUFFED BISON BURGERS WITH BASILCHURRI AND BUTTER LETTUCE BUNS

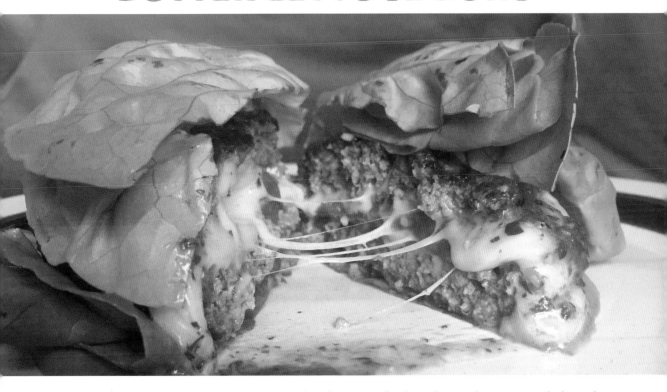

In the summer when my tomatoes are ripe, my family enjoys fresh, Italian-style caprese salad nearly every evening: sliced heirloom tomatoes topped with fresh mozzarella, basil chiffonade, a balsamic and olive oil drizzle, and a bit of sea salt and cracked pepper. This recipe was inspired by our love of this refreshing combination. • **Yield:** 4 (½-pound) burgers | **Prep time:** 10 minutes | **Cook time:** 16 minutes | **Grill/smoker:** charcoal

For the basilchurri

⅓ cup packed finely chopped fresh basil

⅓ cup packed finely chopped fresh parsley

1 tablespoon minced fresh garlic

1 tablespoon lemon juice

1 tablespoon white wine vinegar

½ teaspoon sea salt

pinch of freshly cracked black pepper

pinch of red pepper flakes

3 tablespoons extra virgin olive oil

For the burgers

2 vine-ripe tomatoes, thinly sliced

1 recipe Burger Starter (page 69) using bison, formed into 8 thin (¼-pound) patties

1 cup grated mozzarella cheese

1 head butter lettuce, leaves separated

For the basilchurri

1. In a medium bowl, mix the basil, parsley, garlic, lemon juice, white wine vinegar, sea salt, black pepper, and red pepper flakes.

2. Stir in the olive oil.

3. Stir again prior to serving. Use immediately or store up to 1 day.

For the burgers

1. Place the tomato slices on top of 4 burger patties.

2. Add a quarter cup of cheese on top of each of the 4 patties.

3. Place the remaining 4 patties on top of the patties with tomato and cheese. Seal the edges by pinching the 2 patties together all the way around the burger.

4. Preheat the grill to 375°F or heat coals until they burn white.

5. Place the burgers on the grill. Cook the burgers for about 8 minutes per side, or until they are cooked through to desired doneness.

6. To serve, put 2 or 3 pieces of lettuce together to act as a bottom bun. Top with a burger and a generous drizzle of basilchurri. Top with 2 or 3 more pieces of butter lettuce.

CHEESESTEAK ELK BURGERS

The thing about a real aficionado is they are very particular about what a true Philly cheesesteak is or isn't. Now, while I do love a good cheesesteak, I'm not from Philly. So, to avoid upsetting the masses, I left any origin words out of the name of this particular delight—primarily because I didn't use the traditional store-bought cheese sauce. • *Yield:* 6 (⅓-pound) burgers | *Prep time:* 15 minutes | *Cook time:* 50 minutes | *Grill/smoker:* charcoal

For the peppers and onions

3 tablespoons extra virgin olive oil

2 large white onions, sliced in ¼-inch strips

2½ cups (¼-inch) bell pepper strips, about 3 peppers

½ teaspoon sea salt

For the cheese sauce

4 tablespoons unsalted butter

4 tablespoons all-purpose flour

1 tablespoon chicken bouillon

⅔ cup whipping cream

⅔ cup milk

⅓ cup grated provolone

4 slices American cheese, each cut into 12 pieces

For the burgers

1 recipe Burger Starter (page 69) using elk, divided into 6 patties

6 buns

Garlicky Aioli (page 19)

For the peppers and onions

1. Heat the oil in a large cast-iron skillet over medium-high heat.

2. Add in the onions and peppers, and sprinkle with salt.

3. Cook, flipping the onions and peppers every 3 to 5 minutes to achieve a bit of char, for about 30 minutes, or until the peppers are tender and the onions are limp.

4. Set aside and cover to keep warm.

For the cheese sauce

1. Make a roux by melting the butter in a small saucepan and whisking in the flour over medium heat. Continuously whisk and cook until the mixture has turned a light golden brown, about 3 minutes.

2. Whisk in the chicken bouillon until it is thoroughly incorporated.

3. Slowly stir in the cream and milk and cook for another 2 minutes to bring the mixture back up to heat.

4. Switch the whisk out for a wooden spoon and turn the heat down to medium-low. Slowly stir in the provolone a couple of tablespoons at a time to avoid clumping or drastically affecting the temperature of the sauce.

5. Once the provolone is fully incorporated into the sauce, slowly add in the American cheese pieces, a few at a time, stirring continuously as you did when adding the provolone.

6. Remove the sauce from the heat and cover to keep warm.

For the burgers

1. Bring the grill up to 375°F, or heat the coals until they have turned grayish-white.

2. Lightly oil the grill and place the burgers on the hottest part of the grate.

3. After about 5 minutes, flip the burgers and cook through, about 5 more minutes.

4. Cut the buns in half and lay them face down on the coolest part of the grill grate.

5. Remove the burgers and buns from the grill when the burgers have reached 135°F in the middle, or your desired doneness.

6. To assemble, slather a layer of aioli on both the top and bottom buns. Place the burger atop the bottom bun, pile a portion of peppers and onion on the patty, and drizzle cheese sauce all over the peppers and onions. Add the top bun, and don't forget to supply a lot of napkins for your guests!

Pro Tip: A real cheesesteak sandwich is made with steak—specifically, ribeye. So, you can swap that burger patty out for some tender, thin-sliced, smoked venison rib steak!

VENISON JALAPEÑO POPPER BURGERS

Let's be real, I love fried food. And nothing quite compares to creamy, crunchy, spicy jalapeño poppers. I no longer indulge in this greasy cuisine because I was diagnosed with a gluten allergy. Though it's been over a decade since I have been able to devour a 2000-calorie basket of fried delight, I still crave them on occasion. As such, I bring these flavors into other dishes. My family can't get enough of this one. • *Yield:* 4 (½-pound) burgers | *Prep time:* 10 minutes | *Cook time:* 45 minutes | *Grill/smoker:* pellet grill/smoker

For the stuffing

3 large jalapeños, deseeded, chopped into ¼-inch pieces

8 ounces cream cheese

6 slices bacon, cooked and roughly chopped

¼ teaspoon sea salt

For the burgers

1 recipe Burger Starter (page 69) using venison, divided into 8 (¼-pound) patties

4 buns

4 pieces of cheddar cheese

lettuce, tomato, onion, avocado, and other toppers, to serve, optional

ketchup, mustard, and mayonnaise or Garlicky Aioli (page 19), to serve, optional

For the stuffing

1. Place two thirds of the jalapeños in medium skillet over high heat, stirring occasionally. Use a splatter screen or metal strainer to cover the pan to prevent the jalapeños from popping out of the pan. Cook until the pieces are charred.

2. Warm the cream cheese in a medium saucepan until it is melted and easy to stir.

3. Once the cheese has melted, stir in the bacon, salt, and both the charred and fresh jalapeños.

For the burgers

1. Preheat your grill to 325°F to develop a decent level of smoke.

2. Divide stuffing mix between 4 of the patties, placing it in the center and gently pushing it out toward edges with the back of a spoon. Leave about ½ inch of the edge free from the stuffing. Cover the stuffing with the remaining patties.

3. Seal the edges of the burgers, pinching the 2 patties together around the edges and smoothing the edge with your fingers.

4. Bring smoker temperature down to 130°F and place burgers on the grate. Smoke for 20 minutes and then switch to grilling, bringing temperature back up to 325°F.

5. Grill patties for 5 minutes and flip. Add a slice of cheddar cheese on top of each burger 2 minutes before taking off the grill. Place the patties on hamburger buns and top as desired.

Pro Tip: Looking to cut the carbs back on this burger? Replace the bun with lettuce and gain a nice textural crunch! Use a small head of iceberg lettuce and cut it in half. Pull the small, inner leaves out and reserve them for another use. Leave about 5 leaves from the top half and 5 from the bottom, placing the burger and toppings between.

ANTELOPE BURGER WITH CRISPY SWEET ONIONS, GREEN PEPPER CREAM CHEESE SAUCE, AND PORTOBELLO BUN

With the increase in autoimmune diseases like diabetes and celiac, and dietary trends like paleo and whole 30, there seems to be more interest in "bun" variations. Large portobello mushrooms are a perfect substitution. Though they don't mimic bread, they are a fantastically flavorful vessel for patties and all of their toppings. For a truly guilt-free burger, replace the all-purpose flour with almond or tapioca flour for the crispy onions.

• *Yield:* 6 (⅓-pound) burgers | *Prep time:* 15 minutes | *Cook time:* 20 minutes | *Grill/smoker:* charcoal or natural gas

For the crispy sweet onions

3 tablespoons Perfect Poultry Rub (page 15)

2 tablespoons all-purpose flour

¼ teaspoon sea salt

1 sweet white onion, thinly sliced

unrefined grapeseed oil, or other oil with high smoke point, for frying

For the green pepper cream cheese sauce

½ green pepper

6 ounces cream cheese

2 teaspoons minced fresh garlic

¼ teaspoon freshly cracked black pepper

¼ teaspoon sea salt

For the buns and burgers

¼ cup extra virgin olive oil

¼ cup balsamic vinegar

1 teaspoon onion salt

1 teaspoon garlic powder

1 teaspoon Italian seasoning

12 large portobello mushrooms, gills removed

1 recipe Burger Starter (page 69) using antelope, divided into 6 patties

6 slices cheddar cheese

For the crispy sweet onions

1. Mix the poultry rub, flour, and salt in a zip-top bag.

2. Add the onion to the bag and shake to thoroughly coat with the seasoning mixture.

3. Pour a quarter inch of oil into a medium cast-iron pan and turn the heat to medium-high.

4. Fry the onion slices for approximately 3 minutes per side, or until they are golden brown.

5. Remove the onions from the pan and place them on a paper-lined plate to catch excess oil.

For the green pepper cream cheese sauce

In a blender or food processor, blend the green pepper, cream cheese, garlic, pepper, and salt, and set aside.

For the buns and burgers

1. In a small bowl, mix the oil, vinegar, onion salt, garlic powder, and Italian seasoning together, and paint the mixture over the mushrooms. Make sure the mushrooms are fully coated.

2. Heat the grill to 375°F.

3. Place the burgers and mushrooms on the grill. Flip both after 5 minutes and cook to desired doneness, about 5 more minutes for medium-rare to medium.

4. Add a slice of cheddar cheese on top of each burger 2 minutes before removing them from the grill.

5. To assemble, place a burger patty on top of 1 portobello cap, spoon the green pepper cream cheese sauce atop the patty, cover with crispy sweet onions, and top with another portobello mushroom bun.

Pro Tip: Not in the mood for a burger? Place the cheddar cheese in the mushroom cap and firmly pack the burger mixture in, as well. Smoke it for 1 hour at 200°F. Top with the green pepper cream cheese sauce and crispy onions, and serve with a fork and knife.

GOOSE BURGERS WITH FIG AND BACON JAM AND GOAT CHEESE

Opinions of wild goose meat seem to land on the far ends of the fondness spectrum: You either love it or hate it. Perhaps this is because its flavor is so very unexpected. While it is a poultry variety, it presents closer to a red meat, making it a perfect stand-in for burgers. • *Yield:* 6 (⅓-pound) burgers | *Prep time:* 10 minutes | *Cook time:* 30 to 35 minutes | *Grill/smoker:* charcoal

For the fig and bacon jam

4 ounces (about 4 slices) thick-cut bacon

1 small shallot, minced

1 clove garlic, minced

10 golden figs, roughly chopped

½ cup water

1 tablespoon lemon juice

1 tablespoon maple syrup

pinch of sea salt

pinch of freshly cracked black pepper

1 tablespoon balsamic vinegar

1 teaspoon chopped fresh parsley

For the goose burgers

1 recipe Burger Starter (page 69) using goose meat, divided into 6 (⅓-pound) patties

6 buns

4 ounces goat cheese

1½ cups fresh spinach

For the fig and bacon jam

1. Fry the bacon in a small saucepan over medium heat until crispy, about 6 minutes.

2. Remove the bacon from the pan, chop, and set aside. Do not discard the oil.

3. Using the same pan, sauté the shallot and garlic in the bacon grease until tender, about 5 minutes.

4. Stir in the figs, water, lemon juice, and maple syrup, and turn the heat down to simmer.

5. Simmer, uncovered, for 15 minutes or until the liquid has almost fully evaporated, stirring every 3 to 5 minutes.

6. Stir in the salt, pepper, balsamic vinegar, and parsley, and remove from heat. Serve immediately or cover the jam and store in the refrigerator up to 5 days.

For the goose burgers

1. Bring the grill up to 375°F, or heat the coals until they have burned to white, and place the burger patties on the hottest part of the grill. Cook for 5 minutes per side for a medium-rare to medium burger, or until they reach your desired doneness.

2. Just prior to removing the burgers from the grill, place the buns facedown on the grill to toast.

3. To serve, place the spinach on the bottom bun, then add the burger, the goat cheese, and the fig and bacon jam.

Pro Tip: Use a goat cheese infused with dried fruits, cinnamon, or honey to take this dish from a 10 to an 11.

WILD TURKEY BURGER WITH SWISS CHEESE AND SUN-DRIED TOMATO BASIL SPREAD

Wild turkey gets a bad rap for being dull and dry. Not this burger; it's juicy and flavorful. As with most wild meats, wild turkey needs added fat when making burgers or sausages. I like to add about 15% fat to coarsely ground turkey to achieve a juicy burger that still holds together. How do you keep the breast meat moist without grinding them in fat? If you are planning on smoking or grilling, add a teaspoon of salt to the Perfect Poultry Rub (page 15) and dry brine them overnight. If you aren't set on outdoor cooking your bird, try poaching it in a cream sauce—the results are incredible. • *Yield:* 6 servings | *Prep time:* 10 minutes | *Cook time:* 15 minutes | *Grill/smoker:* charcoal

For the sun-dried tomato spread

⅓ cup sun-dried tomatoes in Italian herbs and oil

1 cup mayo

1 garlic clove

1 small shallot

2 tablespoons chopped fresh basil

For the burgers

1 recipe Burger Starter (page 69) using turkey burger with 15% fat content, formed into ⅓-pound burger patties

6 slices Swiss cheese

6 buns

lettuce and tomato slices, for topping

For the sun-dried tomato spread

Use a blender to combine tomatoes, mayo, garlic, shallot, and basil until a thick paste is formed. Set aside.

For the burgers

1. Preheat the grill to 375°F, or when coals are burning white.

2. Place the burgers on the grill and cook for approximately 7 minutes per side, or until internal temperature has reached 160°F.

3. About 2 minutes before removing the burgers from the grill, add the cheese on top of the burger patties and place the buns facedown on the grate.

4. When the cheese has melted and buns are toasted to a golden brown, remove the burgers and buns from the grill.

5. To assemble, spread the sun-dried tomato spread on the bottom bun, add the burger, and top with fresh tomatoes and lettuce. Add another smear of sun-dried tomato on the top bun before placing it on your masterpiece.

ENCHILADA ELK BURGER WITH GREEN CHILE-CORN CAKE BUN

Made with the Wagyu beef of wild game, this enchilada elk burger is a Mexican twist on a classic beef burger. It's out of this world! The chile–corn cake bun provides that sweet flavor of corn tortilla found in a classic enchilada. Use any extra enchilada sauce to make actual enchiladas or freeze in an air-tight container for up to 3 months. • *Yield:* 8 (¼-pound) burgers | *Prep time:* 20 minutes | *Cook time:* 1 hour 15 minutes | *Grill/smoker:* charcoal

For the corn cake

2 cups fine-ground masa

¼ teaspoon baking powder

3 tablespoons butter

2 large eggs

1 (8.5-ounce) can creamed corn

1 cup grated Colby Jack cheese

1 (4-ounce) can green chiles

⅓ cup pure maple syrup

½ teaspoon sea salt

For the sauce

olive oil, for roasting

14 mixed baby bell peppers or 2 to 3 large bell peppers

1 large jalapeño pepper, or more to taste

1 tablespoon minced fresh garlic (about 3 cloves)

6 ounces tomato paste

1½ cups chicken stock

2 tablespoons dried oregano

1 tablespoon dried ground cumin

1 teaspoon sea salt

½ teaspoon chili powder

For the burgers

1 recipe Burger Starter (page 69) using elk, divided into 8 patties

1 cup shredded cheddar cheese

½ cup sour cream or Cilantro Lime Mayo (page 17)

1 large avocado

2 cups shredded lettuce

½ cup crumbled cotija cheese

¼ cup fresh cilantro leaves, chopped

For the corn cake

1. Preheat the oven to 350°F.

2. Mix the masa and baking powder in a medium bowl.

3. Using a mixer or blender, mix the butter and eggs until there are no butter clumps.

4. Add the egg and butter mixture to the masa a little at a time, whisking to blend thoroughly.

5. Stir in the creamed corn, Colby Jack, green chiles, maple syrup, and sea salt.

6. Divide the mixture into 8 sections and form each into a ball. Flatten each ball slightly to form ½-inch-thick patties.

7. Place the corn cakes on a greased sheet pan, ensuring none are touching.

8. Bake for 25 to 30 minutes or until a toothpick inserted into one of the patties comes out clean. Pull from the oven and let cool.

9. When the corn cake buns have cooled, carefully cut each in half using a sharp bread knife.

For the sauce

1. Preheat the oven to 400°F.

2. Pour olive oil along the bottom of a large cast-iron skillet and add the bell peppers and jalapeño peppers.

3. Drizzle more olive oil on top of the peppers, place the skillet in the oven, and cook for 20 minutes.

4. Flip the peppers and roast for another 20 minutes.

5. Pull the peppers from the oven. While they are still hot, move them to a large bowl and cover it with plastic wrap to steam the peppers. After about 15 minutes of steaming, remove the plastic.

6. Peel the skins off the peppers and remove the seeds and stems.

7. Add the peppers and garlic to a food processor and pulse until smooth.

8. Add in the tomato paste, chicken stock, oregano, cumin, salt, and chili powder. Blend thoroughly.

For the burgers

1. Light the coals and get them burning to white. When the grill is at about 400°F, oil the grate and throw the burger patties on. After 5 minutes, flip the patties.

2. Cook the burgers to rare, 3 to 5 minutes per side, and add the shredded cheddar to melt.

3. When the patties have reached medium-rare and the cheese is melted, pull them from the grill. Slather sour cream on the bottom bun and set the elk patty on top. Top the patty with 2 to 3 tablespoons of enchilada sauce, then avocado, lettuce, cotija cheese, cilantro, and the top half of the bun.

Pro Tip: Make it breakfast! Replace the ground meat in the basic burger recipe with breakfast sausage and top the burger with a fried egg.

CHAPTER SEVEN

Entrées

COCONUT MILK–SOAKED BISON SATAY WITH GINGER PEANUT SAUCE

Historically, bison were a primary source of sustenance for Native American tribes across the plains of North America. Bison is also a much healthier and sustainable alternative to beef. If you were to eat the same size and cut of beef, you would be taking in about 75 percent more fat! • *Yield:* 4 to 5 servings | *Prep time:* 10 minutes, plus 6 hours to marinate | *Cook time:* 5 minutes | *Grill/smoker:* charcoal or pellet

For the bison steak

¼ teaspoon sea salt

¼ teaspoon freshly cracked black pepper

¼ teaspoon ground cumin

¼ teaspoon curry powder

1¼ pounds bison skirt steak

2 (12- to 15-ounce) cans coconut milk

olive oil, for grilling

sesame seeds, for garnish

For the peanut sauce

2 tablespoons sugar

2 tablespoons liquid aminos or coconut aminos

1 tablespoon red wine vinegar

2 tablespoons minced ginger

½ teaspoon garlic powder

½ cup creamy peanut butter

For the bison steak

1. Mix the salt, pepper, cumin, and curry powder in a small bowl. Rub the spice blend all over the bison. Set aside while you prepare the coconut milk.

2. Pour the coconut milk in a deep container that will hold the bison. The coconut milk will likely be separated into coconut cream and coconut water. Mix them together until you have a smooth consistency with no chunks of coconut cream.

3. Slice the steak into pieces about 1 inch wide and 8 inches long. Weave the bison onto skewers.

4. Place the steak skewers in the coconut milk mixture and let sit for 6 hours to overnight for best results.

5. Heat the grill to 325°F.

6. Brush the grill with olive oil and place the steak on for 2 to 3 minutes per side or until the internal temperature has reached your desired doneness. For medium-rare, the meat should reach an internal temperature of 135°F.

For the peanut sauce

1. In a medium bowl, mix all the peanut sauce ingredients together except the peanut butter. Once they are thoroughly mixed, add the peanut butter and mix until smooth.

2. Stir well before use. Drizzle the steak with peanut sauce, and sprinkle sesame seeds on top. Or, serve the sauce in a dish on the side.

Pro Tip: Place Thai Chili Oil (page 18) on the table for guests to add a little heat to their dish. For a fun twist on this dish, add a pineapple slice on each end of the skewer.

CHERRY-SMOKED DUCK WITH HUCKLEBERRY CABERNET SAUCE

This is my favorite dish to serve for an intimate dinner, holiday party, or any time I just really want to impress our guests. Make sure to buy extra bottles of the Cabernet Sauvignon you use in the recipe, as it pairs perfectly with the succulent duck and rich huckleberry sauce. Save any leftover duck for Smoked Duck Fried Rice (page 45) or the Smoked Duck Salad with Goat Cheese, Pecans, and Lemon Maple Vinaigrette (page 38). • *Yield:* 4 to 6 servings | *Prep time:* 20 minutes | *Cook time:* 30 minutes | *Grill/smoker:* electric smoker | *Chips:* cherrywood

For the duck

1 whole (3- to 5-pound) duck, excess fat trimmed and reserved

2 tablespoons minced fresh garlic, divided

3 clementines, peeled

¼ cup pure maple syrup

1 teaspoon sea salt

1 teaspoon dried parsley

1 teaspoon dried rosemary

½ teaspoon chili powder

½ teaspoon nutmeg

¼ teaspoon white pepper

2 teaspoons melted coconut oil

1 teaspoon chopped fresh herbs of choice, for garnish

For the sauce

1 shallot, roughly chopped

¼ teaspoon sea salt

1 teaspoon minced fresh garlic

1¼ cups cabernet

4 ounces huckleberry jam

For the duck

1. Preheat the smoker to 225°F and add in the wood chips.

2. Fill the drip pan with about ¼ inch of water and return it to the smoker.

3. Using cooking twine, tie the legs and wings up tight against the duck's body. Rub 1 tablespoon of garlic in the inside cavity of the bird. Then, stuff the clementines into the cavity.

4. In a small dish, mix together the maple syrup, salt, parsley, rosemary, chili powder, nutmeg, white pepper, remaining tablespoon garlic, and melted coconut oil.

5. Rub the maple syrup mixture all over the bird. Don't forget to get between the legs, wings, body, and any other cracks and crevices.

6. Place the bird in the smoker until the internal temperature reaches 135°F. Pull it out, cover it, and let sit for about 10 minutes. The temperature should rise to 145°F.

For the sauce

1. Render the reserved duck fat by placing it in a small skillet and cooking over low heat until the pieces of fat are slightly crispy and surrounded in fatty liquid.

2. Discard the excess pieces of fat and leave ¼ cup of the rendered fat in the pan.

3. Add in the shallot, salt, and garlic, and sauté on medium-high heat. When the shallots are translucent, add in the wine and turn the heat to simmer. Reduce the wine by half.

4. Add in 4 ounces of huckleberry jam. Continue to cook for another 20 minutes or until the sauce sticks to the back of the spoon.

5. Slice the duck into pieces about ½ inch thick and fan them out on a plate. Drizzle the sauce over (or serve sauce on the side) and top with your favorite chopped herbs.

Pro Tip: Save any excess duck fat for further rendering and use in place of oil or butter to add an extra richness to other recipes. Try tossing vegetables in it and roasting them!

RUSSIAN-STYLE ELK SHASHLIK

The word shashlik comes from the Turkish word for skewer, shish (as in shish kebab). Shashlik is a Russian dish traditionally made with pieces of lamb that have been marinating in onions for several days before being skewered and cooked over an open flame. I find many wild meats share similar flavor properties with lamb, and are really kicked up a notch when they have been soaking in onion juices for several days. • *Yield:* 4 to 6 skewers | *Prep time:* 10 minutes, plus 2 to 3 days to marinate | *Cook time:* 8 minutes | *Grill/smoker:* charcoal or pellet

1 large white onion, thinly sliced

2 teaspoons sea salt

¼ cup pickle juice

1 tablespoon balsamic vinegar

1 teaspoon freshly cracked black pepper

1 teaspoon paprika

½ teaspoon nutmeg

1 pound of elk round steaks, cut into 1-inch cubes

1. Place the onion in a zip-top bag with the salt and let sit for 1 hour.

2. Add in the pickle juice, balsamic vinegar, pepper, paprika, and nutmeg. Ensure that the onions are evenly coated with the ingredients.

3. Add the steak into the bag and mix well.

4. Seal the bag and refrigerate for 2 to 3 days. Mix at least once a day.

5. Remove the meat from the bag, ensuring no onion pieces are stuck to the meat, and thread the meat onto the skewers.

6. Heat the grill to 325°F.

7. Brush the grill with olive oil and place the steak on for 4 minutes per side or until it is cooked to your desired doneness. For medium-rare, the meat should reach an internal temperature of 135°F.

HONEY-SOY DUCK SKEWERS

I don't let any part of the duck go to waste. When piecing the duck, I often remove the breasts and set them aside for cooking whole or stuffing, render the fat to replace oil or butter in recipes, fry the skin to use in place of croutons on salads, and boil the bones for stock. The meat from the legs, wings, and tenders is what I use for curries and skewers. These honey soy skewers are rich, sweet, and salty—and surprisingly easy to make.

• *Yield:* 6 to 8 skewers | *Prep time:* 15 minutes | *Cook time:* 6 minutes | *Grill/smoker:* charcoal or pellet

3 tablespoons preservative-free soy sauce

2 tablespoons honey

leg, wing, and tenderloin meat from duck, cut into ¾-inch pieces

pinch of sea salt

pinch of freshly cracked black pepper

olive oil, for grilling

1. Heat the soy sauce and honey in a small saucepan over low heat until the honey has melted completely and is thoroughly mixed with the soy sauce.

2. Thread the duck onto skewers, sprinkle with salt and pepper, and paint both sides with the honey-soy mixture.

3. Bring the grill up to 375°F or heat the charcoal until coals have turned white.

4. Brush the grill with olive oil and place the skewers on the hottest part of the grate. Brush the skewers with the honey-soy mixture every minute.

5. Flip the skewers after 3 minutes and cook for about another 3 minutes until they reach medium-rare, about 135°F, or desired doneness.

6. Remove the skewers from the grill and serve immediately.

HAWAIIAN-STYLE BOOZY BOOZY DUCK

Huli huli chicken is a staple in Hawaii, known by the sweet and salty ginger sauce slathered over succulent pieces of poultry. But the Hawaiian word huli translates to "turn," referring to the rotisserie style of grilling. While this particular recipe has the same flavor profiles as the island version, the technique is different. Thus, I didn't feel quite right calling it a Huli Huli Duck. Boozy Boozy just kind of rolls off the tongue, though, and seemed quite fitting with the white wine sauce enhancement.

• **Yield:** 4 to 6 servings | **Prep time:** 5 minutes, plus overnight to refrigerate | **Cook time:** 15 to 20 minutes | **Grill/smoker:** charcoal

⅓ cup tamari sauce

1 tablespoon minced fresh garlic

1 tablespoon ginger root paste

½ teaspoon Korean chili paste (gochujang) or sriracha sauce

2 tablespoons molasses

⅓ cup ketchup

1 (20-ounce) can crushed pineapples with juices

1 cup dry white wine

3 pounds duck legs, wings, and thighs

rice, to serve

grilled pineapple, to serve

1. In a large bowl, mix all ingredients together except for the duck, rice, and grilled pineapple.

2. Add the duck to the bowl and mix to coat well. Let it sit in the refrigerator overnight. Before grilling, reserve the marinade.

3. The preferred huli huli cooking method is over an open flame (rotisserie-style), so I use a charcoal grill. When the temperature is around 400 to 425°F or the coals are white, oil the grill and place the duck directly on the grate for 6 to 8 minutes per side or until the internal temperature reaches 140°F.

4. Place the reserved marinade in a small cast-iron grill pan. Place the pan on the grill and let it slightly caramelize, stirring frequently to avoid burning.

5. Remove the duck from the grill and let sit for 2 to 5 minutes, covered, before serving. To serve, drizzle the sauce over the duck and serve over rice or alongside grilled pineapple.

Pro Tip: Make it a true Huli Huli Duck. Leave the bird whole and use a rotisserie spit (you can purchase motorized rotisserie kits for most grill types). Slather it with the sauce every 10 minutes, using a basting brush or mop. It should take about 1 hour to cook but check the temperature with a meat thermometer to ensure optimal doneness.

SMOKED CIDER BRAISED QUAIL

The marvel of this dish comes from the fact that the level of delectableness matches that of the entertainment facet. Quail looks like a skinny little single-serving chicken, and it's so fun to eat. My young daughter loves to dance her bird across the plate prior to savoring each sweet, tender bite.

• *Yield:* 4 servings | *Prep time:* 10 minutes | *Cook time:* 1 hour | *Grill/smoker:* electric smoker | *Chips:* applewood

1 (12-ounce) can hard-hopped cider

¼ teaspoon turmeric

1 teaspoon onion powder

1½ teaspoons dried parsley

½ teaspoon Hungarian sweet paprika

¼ teaspoon cinnamon

¼ teaspoon ground mustard seed

¼ teaspoon freshly cracked black pepper

¼ teaspoon ground red pepper

½ teaspoon allspice

½ teaspoon sea salt

½ teaspoon dried rosemary

½ teaspoon dried oregano

4 whole quail (approximately 4 ounces each), mostly deboned

greens, rice, or pasta, for serving

fresh herbs, for garnish

1. Heat your smoker to 250°F and add in chips.

2. Mix all ingredients together except the quail, greens, and garnish. Use a whisk to ensure the dry ingredients are well blended into the liquid. Pour the mixture into the smoker's drip pan or a shallow cast-iron pan, if not using the electric smoker.

3. Line the quail up along the bottom of the pan so they are swimming in the apple cider mixture.

4. Smoke the quail for 1 hour or until the internal temperature has reached 160°F.

5. Remove the quail from the smoker, cover, and let sit for 5 minutes before serving. Serve whole atop a bed of greens, rice, or pasta. Garnish with fresh herbs.

Pro Tip: I prefer a braised quail because it produces a moist bird every time, and quail easily dries out. However, if you're looking for a crispy skin and rich color, marinate the quail overnight in a sealed container or zip-top storage bag. Discard half of the marinating liquid and mix the other half with ½ cup of oil. Brush the mixture over the bird and place it on the smoker at 225°F for 1½ to 2 hours (or until 160°F internal temperature has been reached), brushing the liquid on the bird every 15 minutes.

HICKORY-SMOKED MAPLE RABBIT

When I come across folks who are hesitant to try something new or who proclaim they don't like a particular dish or ingredient, I consider it a challenge. I truly believe with willingness, an open mind, and proper preparation, anything can be turned into a scrumptious treat. Absolutely everyone I have served rabbit to has changed their opinion about eating "bunny"—and that is especially true when I serve Hickory-Smoked Maple Rabbit. • *Yield:* 4 to 6 servings | *Prep time:* 5 minutes | *Cook time:* 3 hours | *Grill/smoker:* electric or pellet smoker | *Chips:* hickory

1 teaspoon onion powder

1 teaspoon minced fresh garlic

¼ teaspoon garlic salt

½ cup pure maple syrup

1 teaspoon dried parsley flakes

½ teaspoon Hungarian sweet paprika

¼ teaspoon freshly cracked black pepper

¼ teaspoon ground red pepper

¼ teaspoon celery salt

1 (3-pound) rabbit

salad greens, cooked rice, or pasta, to serve

1. Heat the electric smoker to 165°F, fill the steam pan with ½ inch of water, and add in the wood chips.

2. In a medium bowl, whisk together the onion powder, fresh garlic, garlic salt, maple syrup, parsley, paprika, black pepper, red pepper, and salt.

3. Rub the mixture all over the rabbit, massaging it in thoroughly.

4. Place the rabbit in the smoker, directly over the drip pan. Smoke for 2 hours and turn the temperature up to 300°F.

5. Cook for 1 more hour or until internal temperature has reached 160°F.

6. Pull from the smoker, cover, and let sit for 5 minutes before serving. Serve whole atop a bed of greens, rice, or pasta.

Pro Tip: About 30 minutes before pulling the meat from the smoker, paint barbecue sauce all over the rabbit, flip, and do the same on the other side. Serve with extra barbecue sauce for dipping.

CHERRY-GLAZED WHOLE SMOKED PHEASANT WITH CORNBREAD STUFFING

Growing up, certain debates occurred annually at holiday meals. For Christmas Eve, it was whether we needed to have clam chowder or oyster stew; Christmas, turkey or ham; but the mother of all holiday discussions came on Thanksgiving. Should we have traditional white-bread stuffing or Southern-style cornbread stuffing, and is it better in or out of the bird? Backing down is a trait that no one in my family possesses, so instead, we prepared both and ate it for a week. For the record, I prefer cornbread stuffing bursting out of the cavity of the bird. Here, I use pheasant basted in a cherry wine glaze so every piece of meat is tender and flavorful. • *Yield:* 4 servings | *Prep time:* 25 minutes, plus 12 hours to refrigerate | *Cook time:* 2 hours 50 minutes to 3 hours 50 minutes | *Grill/smoker:* electric smoker or pellet | *Chips:* cherrywood

For the stuffing

1 (15-ounce) box cornbread mix, baked according to package instruction, cut into ¾-inch cubes

3 tablespoons olive oil

2 tablespoons minced fresh sage

4 tablespoons unsalted butter

2 celery sticks, chopped

1 large carrot, peeled and chopped

1 small white onion, chopped

1 garlic clove, roughly chopped

½ teaspoon sea salt

½ teaspoon freshly cracked black pepper

¼ cup water

1½ cups milk

2 tablespoons chicken bouillon

1 tablespoon Perfect Poultry Rub (page 15)

For the pheasant

1 whole pheasant

2 to 3 tablespoons Perfect Poultry Rub (page 15)

1 teaspoon sea salt

½ cup cherry pie filling

¼ cup light-bodied red wine

For the stuffing

1. Preheat the oven to 350°F.

2. Spread the cornbread cubes on a sheet pan and toss them in the oil and sage. Bake for 15 minutes, flip, and bake for 15 more minutes. Pull out and set aside.

3. Melt the butter in a large saucepan. Add in the celery, carrot, and onion, and cook over medium heat for about 8 minutes, or until soft.

4. Stir in the garlic, salt, pepper, and water, and simmer for 10 more minutes.

5. Stir in the milk, bouillon, and poultry seasoning, and stir to combine. Then add the cornbread croutons and toss gently until all liquid is absorbed.

For the pheasant

1. Massage the outside of the pheasant with the poultry rub and salt and refrigerate for at least 12 hours.

2. Stuff the cavity of the bird with the stuffing and tie the legs and wings tight to the body using cooking twine.

3. Bring smoker up to 170°F and smoke the bird for 1 hour.

4. While the bird is smoking, puree the cherry pie filling and wine in a blender.

6. Reserve enough stuffing to fill the cavity of the bird. The remaining stuffing should be placed in a covered, oven-safe dish and baked at 350°F for 20 minutes. This can be served alongside the bird or stored for a later meal.

5. After the first hour of smoking, baste the bird with the cherry glaze every half hour until the internal temperature reaches 160°F, or for another 1 to 2 hours. Then remove the bird from the smoker and let rest for 10 minutes prior to carving.

6. To serve, untie the wings and legs, carve as desired, and spoon out the warm stuffing to serve as a side.

BISON BULGOGI

The popular sweet, salty, thin-sliced Korean beef dish called bulgogi translates to "fire meat," which speaks to its method of cooking. My variation is a re-creation of a family favorite that dates back to my childhood, more than 20 years before I learned the proper pronunciation of the dish. • *Yield:* 4 to 6 servings | *Prep time:* 4½ hours | *Cook time:* 6 to 10 minutes | *Grill/smoker:* charcoal

¾ cup tamari sauce

¼ cup pure sesame oil

½ cup agave nectar

1 tablespoon minced fresh ginger

1 tablespoon minced fresh garlic

1 teaspoon onion powder

2 tablespoons Worcestershire sauce

½ teaspoon freshly cracked black pepper

1 teaspoon black sesame seeds, plus more for garnish

1 teaspoon white sesame seeds, plus more for garnish

1½ pounds bison flank steak, sliced into ¼- to ½-inch strips

1 bunch green onions, greens and whites sliced in ¼-inch pieces

salad greens or cooked rice or pasta, to serve

1. In a large bowl, mix the tamari, sesame oil, agave nectar, ginger, garlic, onion powder, Worcestershire sauce, pepper, black sesame seeds, and white sesame seeds.

2. Add the meat to the mixture. Cover the entire mixture and refrigerate it from 4 hours to overnight.

3. When ready to cook, place the grill grate as far from the fire as possible and add coals.

4. Once the coals are completely white, gently place the marinated meat on the grill, taking care not to drop them through the grate and onto the fire. Cook for approximately 3 minutes per side.

5. Pull from the grill and sprinkle with additional sesame seeds and chopped green onions. Serve atop a bed of greens, rice, or pasta.

Pro Tip: Kick up the heat a bit by replacing the pure sesame oil with the Thai Chili Oil (page 18).

GRILLED BACON-WRAPPED MEATLOAF TOPPED WITH WHITE CHEDDAR MASHED POTATOES

I've never been a fan of meatloaf. But I do think the base ingredients are pretty great—ground meat, onions, and egg. So why not make this classic dish shine and change the perception? I started by upping the quality of the meat with some elk burger, utilizing pulverized pretzels in place of white bread, wrapped the whole thing in bacon, donned the grand creation with creamy, white cheddar mashed Yukon gold potatoes, and of course, threw it on the grill! Serve alongside your favorite vegetable side dish. • **Yield:** 4 servings | **Prep time:** 15 minutes | **Cook time:** 40 minutes | **Grill/smoker:** charcoal, pellet, or gas

For the white cheddar mashed potatoes

2 large Yukon gold potatoes, peeled and cut into 1-inch pieces

¼ teaspoon sea salt

1 tablespoon unsalted butter

3 tablespoons milk

⅓ cup heavy whipping cream

2 ounces white cheddar, grated

For the meatloaf

2 tablespoons olive oil

1 small white onion, chopped

1 large carrot, grated

¾ teaspoon sea salt

1 large egg

¼ cup crushed pretzels

1 pound ground elk or other ground venison

2 tablespoons minced fresh garlic

½ teaspoon dried basil flakes

1 teaspoon dried, crushed rosemary

½ teaspoon freshly cracked black pepper

1 tablespoon Worcestershire sauce

4 slices thick-cut smoked bacon

For the white cheddar mashed potatoes

1. Place the potatoes in a medium pot and fill with water. Add salt to the water and bring to a boil.

2. Keep the water boiling for about 10 minutes or until the potatoes can be easily pierced with a fork.

3. Drain the potatoes and return them to the pot.

4. Add in the butter and milk, and mix with a hand mixer until the potatoes are smooth.

5. Add the cream and turn the heat to low, frequently stirring and scraping the bottom so it doesn't scorch.

6. When the potatoes start to bubble, turn off the heat and stir in the cheese.

7. Place the mashed potatoes in the piping bag.

For the meatloaf

1. In a medium skillet, cook the onion and carrot in 2 tablespoons of olive oil over medium heat until the onions are translucent, about 10 minutes.

2. In a large bowl, whisk the salt and egg together. When fully combined, mix in the pretzels.

3. Add the meat, garlic, basil, rosemary, pepper, Worcestershire, and onion mixture to the bowl, and mix thoroughly.

4. Divide the mixture in quarters and form four 2-inch-thick patties.

5. Wrap a slice of bacon around the diameter of each patty and secure it with a toothpick.

6. Heat your grill up to 300°F or heat the charcoal until the outside of the charcoal has turned white and place the mini meatloaves on the hottest part of the grill.

7. Cook each meatloaf for 10 minutes and flip, moving them to the coolest spot of the grill.

8. Pipe the mashed potatoes on top of each meatloaf, making a circle on the outer edge of the meatloaf and filling it in, much as you would with soft-serve ice cream.

9. Cook for another 20 minutes with the grill cover closed.

SPAGHETTI WITH MONTANA MEATBALL AND MUSHROOM SKEWERS

Yes, I said earlier that spaghetti is a mainstay in venison cooking and that too often, the venison is reserved for beef substitutions in dishes that cover up a meat's unique flavor. I'm not a hypocrite, I promise. The dishes I mentioned are all delightful comfort foods that I often crave, but when making them with venison, I bring the flavor of the meat to the forefront, rather than covering it up, as is often the case in venison applications. • *Yield:* 6 servings | *Prep time:* 10 minutes plus 30 minutes to marinate | *Cook time:* 60 minutes | *Grill/smoker:* charcoal or propane

1 teaspoon sea salt

1 small yellow onion, chopped in ½-inch pieces

2 large carrots, cut into ¼-inch rounds

olive oil, for sautéing

1 pound sweet Italian sausage

2 tablespoons minced fresh garlic

1 large red pepper, cut into ¾-inch chunks

1 (6-ounce) can tomato paste

1 (30-ounce) can diced tomatoes

½ teaspoon lavender

1 tablespoon Italian seasoning blend

1 large whole bay leaf

½ teaspoon white pepper

½ teaspoon paprika

1 pound cremini or white button mushrooms

8 ounces Italian dressing

12 ounces dried spaghetti

Montana Meatballs (page 25), seared but not cooked

grated Parmesan cheese or truffle oil, to serve

1. Sprinkle sea salt over onion and carrots. Add the salted vegetables to a saucepan along with olive oil, and sauté over medium-high heat.

2. When onion is translucent, add Italian sausage, garlic, and red pepper.

3. When sausage is cooked, turn down heat and add the tomato paste, diced tomatoes, lavender, Italian seasoning, bay leaf, white pepper, and paprika. Simmer for 45 minutes.

4. While the sauce is cooking, soak the mushrooms in Italian dressing for approximately 30 minutes in the refrigerator.

5. To prepare the skewers, alternate meatballs and mushrooms on each skewer until the skewers are filled.

6. Bring grill to about 250°F or heat the charcoal until the outer coating of the charcoal has turned white, and place skewers on it. Cook them for about 3 to 5 minutes on each side.

7. Place a pot of hot water on the stove while skewers are grilling. Add 1 teaspoon of salt to the water and bring to boil. When water is boiling, add the noodles and stir.

8. Remove the noodles from the heat when al dente and drain the water, reserving about 2 tablespoons.

9. Add the sauce to the noodles and mix in the saved pasta water.

10. To serve, place 1 to 2 skewers on top of a mound of spaghetti and sauce. Top with Parmesan cheese, truffle oil, or whatever your heart desires!

Pro Tip: If you don't have metal skewers, no problem! Just make sure you soak the bamboo skewers in water (or red wine) for about 30 minutes before skewering the meatballs and mushrooms.

CHERMOULA SPICED RABBIT WITH ROASTED PEPPER CHUTNEY

I've never been to Morocco but there are three reasons it has entered the top 5 of my travel bucket list: the imperial cities, the beaches, and (obviously) the food. The North African spice blend, chermoula, is refreshing, melding an exotic depth and warmth into the dishes it graces. In Morocco, chermoula is primarily used to enhance fish recipes, though it's also great when incorporated into other meat and vegetable dishes. Of course, I had to test its limits and see how it impacted grilled rabbit. The results? Well, it made it into this cookbook, didn't it? • *Yield:* 4 to 6 servings | *Prep time:* 15 minutes, plus 30 minutes to sit | *Cook time:* 2 hours 25 minutes | *Grill/smoker:* natural gas or charcoal

For the chutney

4 tablespoons butter, divided

½ red onion, roughly chopped

1 clove garlic, minced

pinch of sea salt

1 large red pepper, roasted and chopped

2 tablespoons white balsamic vinegar

¼ teaspoon cinnamon

¼ teaspoon cardamom

pinch of freshly cracked black pepper

pinch of crushed red pepper

3 tablespoons water

2 tablespoons brown sugar

For the rabbit

¼ teaspoon saffron threads

2 tablespoons water

1 teaspoon garlic powder

½ teaspoon cumin

½ teaspoon turmeric

½ teaspoon sea salt

¼ teaspoon paprika

¼ teaspoon onion powder

¼ teaspoon crushed red pepper

¼ teaspoon freshly cracked black pepper

¼ teaspoon allspice

¼ teaspoon grated nutmeg

¼ teaspoon ground Ceylon cinnamon

¼ teaspoon ground cardamom

½ cup olive oil

1 bunch flat-leafed parsley, stems removed, finely chopped

¼ cup packed finely chopped fresh cilantro

1 whole rabbit

3 tablespoons melted butter, for basting

For the chutney

1. Melt 2 tablespoons of butter in a small saucepan and add the onion and garlic. Sprinkle with salt and cook on medium low for 10 minutes, or until the onions have turned translucent.

2. Stir in the roasted red pepper, vinegar, cinnamon, cardamom, cracked pepper, red pepper flakes, and water, and simmer for 20 minutes.

3. Stir in the brown sugar and remaining butter, and cook for an additional 5 minutes.

For the rabbit

1. Drop the saffron threads in a small dish and slightly crush them with the back of a spoon. Add in the water and let sit for at least 30 minutes.

2. In another, mid-sized dish, mix the garlic powder, cumin, turmeric, sea salt, paprika, onion powder, crushed red pepper, black pepper, allspice, nutmeg, cinnamon, and cardamom.

3. Stir in the olive oil, parsley, cilantro, and saffron/water mixture.

4. Massage the mixture all over the rabbit, lifting legs to get underneath, and coating the inside of the body cavity.

5. Heat the grill to 375°F or heat the charcoal until coals turn white, and brush oil over the grate.

6. Place the whole rabbit on the grill. Cook with the lid closed for about 1 hour, occasionally basting with butter. Flip and cook another hour on the other side, or until cooked through to 160°F. If using a charcoal grill, you will likely need to add coals at some point.

7. To serve, carve the rabbit and top with the chutney, or serve the chutney on the side.

Pro Tip: Chermoula contains magnificent multipurpose flavor. Why stop at rabbit? Try it on fish, goose, pork, and chicken; drizzle it over skewers; or utilize it in simple rice dishes and serve as a side to smoked meats.

CHAR-GRILLED VENISON TACOS WITH SIMPLE MANGO SALSA AND CILANTRO LIME MAYO

Tacos are a go-to meal when we are overly busy with work, school, farm, and household activities. My tacos are much tastier than the Americanized classic of ground beef, cheddar cheese, and iceberg lettuce! While my version is more of a fusion than the truly authentic variety, they are always loaded with contrasting flavors of savory, tart, and sweet—characteristics often found in authentic tacos. The sweet mango in this recipe provides the perfect balance to the spicy, charred chiles and smoky venison, and the lime mayo encourages a melding of flavors. Serve with a salty, white cheese like cotija, feta, or aged white cheddar. • *Yield:* 10 tacos | *Prep time:* 15 minutes | *Cook time:* 10 to 15 minutes | *Grill/ smoker:* charcoal or natural gas

For the mango salsa

1 large green chile pepper (Anaheim, poblano, or other of preferred heat)

1 whole mango, cut into ¾-inch cubes

1 cup coarsely chopped cilantro

2 tablespoons lime juice

½ teaspoon ground cumin

sea salt and freshly cracked black pepper, to taste

For the venison tacos

½ teaspoon cumin

¼ teaspoon chili powder

¼ teaspoon cinnamon

¼ teaspoon celery salt

1 teaspoon oregano

1 teaspoon garlic powder

¼ teaspoon paprika

pinch of red pepper

pinch of white pepper

1 pound round deer steak

1 tablespoon olive oil

2 tablespoon orange juice

10 corn tortillas

Cilantro Lime Mayo (page 17), to serve

4 to 6 ounces salty, white cheese, to serve

For the mango salsa

1. Turn your gas grill to the highest setting or, if using charcoal, heat coals to their hottest point. Flame-roast the green chile pepper directly over the hottest part of the grill, turning every 3 to 5 minutes to char all sides.

2. Remove the roasted chile pepper and place it in a covered bowl. Let the pepper steam for 10 minutes. Then, remove the seeds and stems, and chop into ¼-inch pieces.

3. In a medium bowl, add the chopped pepper, mango, cilantro, lime juice, cumin, salt, and pepper, mix, and set in the refrigerator or cooler while you prepare the meat.

For the tacos

1. In a medium bowl, mix the cumin, chili powder, cinnamon, celery salt, oregano, garlic powder, paprika, red pepper, and white pepper. Then, rub the spice blend all over the meat. Toss the meat in olive oil and orange juice. Let it sit for 5 to 10 minutes.

2. Heat the grill to approximately 350°F, add the meat, and sear the first side until grill marks appear.

3. Flip and cook on remaining side to desired doneness. For rare to medium-rare, the internal temperature should reach between 130 and 135°F. Cover and let sit for 5 minutes. The meat will continue to cook.

4. While the meat is sitting, place the tortillas on the grill for about 1 minute per side. Remove from the grill and set aside.

5. Smear the Cilantro Lime Mayo over each tortilla, then top with meat, mango salsa, and crumbled cheese.

CHAPTER EIGHT

Jerky and Sausage

OLD-FASHIONED JERKY

Good, old-fashioned jerky—it continues to present itself on menus of meat shops, at grocery store checkouts, and in every at-home processor's bag of jerky tricks. That said, though the typical flavor profile remains the same from recipe to recipe, each seems to have a secret ingredient. Soon, you'll know mine. • *Yield:* 1½ pounds | *Prep time:* 15 minutes, plus 2 to 3 days to marinate | *Cook time:* 5 to 8 hours | *Grill/smoker:* electric smoker | *Chips:* mesquite or hickory

½ cup frozen orange juice concentrate, thawed

⅓ cup vegetable oil

⅓ cup preservative-free soy sauce or tamari

¼ cup Worcestershire sauce

¼ cup liquid smoke

¼ cup packed brown sugar

1 tablespoon minced fresh garlic

1 teaspoon onion salt

½ teaspoon paprika

3 pounds venison, pronghorn, or other meat, sliced against the grain into ¼- to ½-inch strips

1. Thoroughly mix all ingredients except the meat in a large bowl.

2. Add the meat to the bowl and stir until well coated.

3. Cover and refrigerate for 2 to 3 days, turning a couple of times a day.

4. Bring the smoker up to 160°F and place the strips of meat on the grate, leaving a small amount of space between each strip so they aren't touching. After 5 hours, check the jerky. At this point, some of the more thinly sliced pieces or those closest to the heat source might be done. They should feel dry on the outside but still have a bit of moisture in the center. Remove those pieces and return the rest to the smoker to finish, which should take approximately 1 to 3 additional hours. Check occasionally throughout the remaining cook time.

HICKORY HONEY JERKY

The bold smoke released from hickory wood helps intensify the natural sweetness in honey, creating a really nice balance in this protein-packed snack. The extraordinary ingredient in this jerky recipe isn't the honey, though. It's allspice, the aromatic berries from a species of evergreen tree. • *Yield:* 1½ pounds | *Prep time:* 15 minutes, plus 2 to 3 days to marinate | *Cook time:* 5 to 8 hours | *Grill/smoker:* electric smoker | *Chips:* hickory

¼ cup honey

¼ cup coconut aminos

¼ cup white wine vinegar

2 tablespoons olive oil

1 tablespoon Dijon mustard

1 tablespoon ketchup

1 tablespoon paprika

1 tablespoon freshly cracked black pepper

¾ teaspoon allspice

Follow the recipe for Old-Fashioned Jerky on page 119, replacing the seasonings with the ingredients listed above.

APPLE-SMOKED MAPLE AND BROWN SUGAR JERKY

Applewood is a classic wood choice for smoking bacon and tenderloin but is often overlooked when it comes to making jerky—likely due to its intense smoke levels and the long smoke. However, that intensely sweet smoke pairs beautifully with maple and brown sugar in this jerky application. • *Yield:* 1½ pounds | *Prep time:* 15 minutes, plus 2 to 3 days to marinate | *Cook time:* 5 to 8 hours | *Grill/smoker:* electric smoker | *Chips:* applewood

½ cup packed brown sugar

½ cup pure maple syrup

¼ cup preservative-free soy sauce

¼ cup coconut oil

½ cup spiced apple cider

½ teaspoon paprika

2 tablespoons balsamic vinegar

1 teaspoon garlic salt

pinch of Korean-style chili flakes (gochugaru), or to taste

Follow the recipe for Old-Fashioned Jerky on page 119, replacing the seasonings with the ingredients listed above.

SWEET AND SPICY JERKY

This is my favorite jerky recipe in the book. If you like good levels of heat that won't send you into a frantic hunt for a glass of milk to cool your mouth after each bite, this might be the recipe for you.
• *Yield:* 1½ pounds | *Prep time:* 15 minutes, plus 2 to 3 days to marinate | *Cook time:* 5 to 8 hours |
Grill/smoker: electric smoker | *Chips:* mesquite or hickory

½ cup hard apple cider

2 tablespoons Korean chili paste (gochujang)

1 tablespoon onion powder

1 tablespoon Worcestershire sauce

1 tablespoon preservative-free soy sauce

1 tablespoon hot chili oil

1 tablespoon apple cider vinegar

1 tablespoon packed brown sugar

1½ teaspoons dried basil flakes

1 teaspoon garlic salt

¼ teaspoon crushed red pepper

¼ teaspoon chili powder

3 pounds venison, rabbit, or goose, sliced against the grain into ¼- to ½-inch strips

Follow the recipe for Old-Fashioned Jerky on page 119, replacing the seasonings and meat with the ingredients listed above.

CITRUS-THYME JERKY

While this particular marinade is great on venison, the refreshing citrus and fragrant thyme are a wonderful application for those other meats you've been dying to turn into jerky—rabbit, goose, duck, and even 'gator. • *Yield:* 1½ pounds | *Prep time:* 15 minutes, plus 2 to 3 days to marinate | *Cook time:* 5 to 8 hours | *Grill/smoker:* electric smoker | *Chips:* alderwood

⅔ cup orange juice concentrate

1 fresh lemon, juiced

2 tablespoons chopped fresh thyme

1 teaspoon onion salt

1 teaspoon lemon pepper

1 teaspoon fish sauce

1 teaspoon paprika

Follow the recipe for Old-Fashioned Jerky on page 119, replacing the seasonings with the ingredients listed above.

CHIPOTLE MOLE JERKY

Mole is made using unsweetened cocoa, which is actually pretty bitter and a far cry from its popular sugar-infused cousin. When accompanied by traditional Mexican ingredients like tomatoes and peppers, you get a smooth yet bold concoction. • *Yield:* 1½ pounds | *Prep time:* 15 minutes, plus 2 to 3 days to marinate |

Cook time: 5 to 8 hours | *Grill/smoker:* electric smoker | *Chips:* mesquite

1 (7-ounce) can chipotle chiles in juice, puréed in blender

1 (6-ounce) can tomato paste

½ cup water

2 tablespoons dark, unsweetened cocoa powder

1 cup simple syrup

½ cup oil

2 tablespoons minced fresh garlic

1 tablespoon onion salt

1½ teaspoons ground cumin

1½ teaspoons ground Ceylon cinnamon

Follow the recipe for Old-Fashioned Jerky on page 119, replacing the seasonings with the ingredients listed above.

GREEN CHILE–CILANTRO WITH LIME JERKY

I'm a sucker for green chiles, cilantro, and lime. Lime infuses a mild tanginess into the meat that perfectly balances the green chiles and is rounded out with the cilantro and garlic salt. • *Yield:* 1½ pounds | *Prep time:* 15 minutes, plus 2 to 3 days to marinate | *Cook time:* 5 to 8 hours | *Grill/smoker:* electric smoker | *Chips:* mesquite

1 bunch fresh cilantro, stems removed

1 (4-ounce) can mild green chiles with juices

⅔ cup lime juice

⅓ cup avocado oil

2 teaspoons garlic salt

2 teaspoons adobo seasoning

2 teaspoons freshly cracked black pepper

1 teaspoon cumin

3 pounds venison, poultry, or rabbit, sliced against the grain into ¼- to ½-inch strips

Use a blender to puree the first eight ingredients above, then pour the mixture over the meat in a large bowl, stirring to coat well.

Follow steps 3 and 4 for Old-Fashioned Jerky on page 119.

SESAME SOY JERKY

Asian flavors are great in jerky marinades but they are usually prepared as a sweet teriyaki. This recipe, however, is very low in sugar content while still melding many other Asian flavors into an incredibly tasty meat treat. • *Yield:* 1½ pounds | *Prep time:* 15 minutes, plus 2 to 3 days to marinate | *Cook time:* 5 to 8 hours | *Grill/smoker:* electric smoker | *Chips:* alderwood

½ cup preservative-free soy sauce

¼ cup plus 2 tablespoons pure, toasted sesame oil

¼ cup rice vinegar

1 teaspoon Chinese five-spice

1 tablespooon onion powder

½ teaspoon grated fresh ginger

1 teaspoon garlic salt

Follow the recipe for Old-Fashioned Jerky on page 119, replacing the seasonings with the ingredients listed above. After placing the meat in the grate in step 4, sprinkle black and white sesame seeds on both sides of the jerky.

WHISKEY AND SPICED CIDER JERKY

Carry this in your backpack for your next hunting or hiking trip for a protein pick-me-up on the go. Or, pass the bag around the campfire to share with friends. • *Yield:* 1½ pounds | *Prep time:* 15 minutes, plus 2 to 3 days to marinate | *Cook time:* 5 to 8 hours | *Grill/smoker:* electric smoker | *Chips:* mesquite

1 cup sour mash whiskey

2 cups spiced apple cider

2 tablespoons apple cider vinegar

1½ tablespoons finely chopped ginger

½ cup olive oil

2¼ teaspoons celery salt

½ teaspoon cardamom

1 teaspoon cinnamon

½ teaspoon allspice

¼ teaspoon red pepper

1 teaspoon minced fresh garlic

1 (21-gram) package spiced apple cider powder

3 pounds venison, sliced against the grain into ¼-inch strips

Follow the recipe for Old-Fashioned Jerky on page 119, replacing the seasonings and meat with the ingredients listed above.

BOURBON PEACH JERKY

While attending college in the Florida Panhandle, I developed a fondness for the combination of oaky bourbon and sweet peaches. When it occurred to me to marinate my favorite snack food in this mixture, I was convinced I might be a culinary genius. After trying this recipe, you might just agree.
• *Yield:* 1½ pounds | *Prep time:* 15 minutes, plus 2 to 3 days to marinate | *Cook time:* 5 to 8 hours | *Grill/smoker:* electric smoker | *Chips:* alderwood

1½ cups bourbon

2 cups peach juice

½ cup packed brown sugar

¼ cup sweet preservative-free soy sauce

1 tablespoon minced fresh garlic

1 tablespoon onion powder

1 teaspoon cinnamon

1 teaspoon celery salt

1 teaspoon freshly cracked black pepper

1 teaspoon nutmeg

3 pounds venison, sliced, against the grain, into ½-inch strips

Follow the recipe for Old-Fashioned Jerky on page 119, replacing the seasonings and meat with the ingredients listed above.

GARLIC, CRACKED PEPPER, AND SEA SALT JERKY

This jerky has enough garlic to ward off vampires, sending them back to their coffins for the rest of eternity. There's a decent amount of sea salt and black pepper in the marinade, but I also recommend adding some sea salt crystals and freshly cracked black pepper after placing it on the smoker grates.
• *Yield:* 1½ pounds | *Prep time:* 15 minutes, plus 2 to 3 days to marinate | *Cook time:* 5 to 8 hours | *Grill/smoker:* electric smoker | *Chips:* alderwood

⅔ cup fresh garlic paste

⅓ cup extra virgin olive oil

½ tablespoon sea salt, plus more for sprinkling

½ teaspoon freshly cracked black pepper, plus more for grinding over top

Follow the recipe for Old-Fashioned Jerky on page 119, replacing the seasonings and meat with the ingredients listed above. After placing the meat in the grate in step 4, sprinkle more sea salt and freshly cracked black pepper on both sides of the jerky.

BLACK BEAR PEMMICAN WITH DRIED FRUIT AND NUTS

You might want to consider doubling or tripling this recipe. It's that good—like a meaty granola bar without the carbs. There's a certain richness in bear meat that pairs incredibly well with the dried sweet fruits, and the nuts add an unexpected crunch. This recipe also works well with any type of venison. • *Yield:* 1½ pounds | *Prep time:* 30 minutes | *Cook time:* 5 to 7 hours | *Grill/smoker:* electric smoker or pellet | *Chips:* cherrywood

3 pounds 50/50 ground black bear and pork

2 tablespoons liquid smoke

2 tablespoons minced fresh garlic

1 tablespoon minced fresh ginger

1 tablespoon onion powder

1 tablespoon seasoning salt

1½ teaspoons dried sage

1 teaspoon freshly cracked black pepper

1 teaspoon ground nutmeg

½ teaspoon tamari

⅓ cup pecans, chopped

⅓ cup almond pieces, chopped

¼ cup dried dates, chopped

¼ cup dried cranberries, chopped

1. In a large bowl, mix the ground meat, liquid smoke, garlic, ginger, onion powder, seasoning salt, sage, pepper, nutmeg, and tamari, until thoroughly combined.

2. Fold in the pecans, almonds, dates, and cranberries.

3. Preheat the oven to 170°F. Cover the inside of a 13 x 9-inch baking pan with parchment pepper.

4. Press the meat mixture firmly into the pan and smooth the top so the mixture is evenly distributed.

5. Use convection bake to cook the pemmican for 1 hour. If you do not have a convection oven, turn the heat up to 200°F and leave the door open, turning the pan halfway through the cooking process.

6. While the meat is cooking in the oven, bring the temperature of the smoker up to 160°F.

7. Remove the meat from the oven. Make a slice all the way down the middle, lengthwise. Then, turn the pan and cut strips approximately ¼ inch wide.

8. Remove the grates from the smoker. Carefully remove the strips of the meat from the pan and place them on the grate, leaving a small amount of space between each strip so they aren't touching.

9. Return the grates to the smoker and smoke the pemmican for 4 to 6 hours, or until it is dry yet tender.

Pro Tip: Try variations of this recipe. Include multiple types of dried fruit, nuts, seeds, and grains. No bear meat? No problem. This recipe works well with venison and beef.

ELK AND PRONGHORN SMOKED SUMMER SAUSAGE

Summer sausage is an incredible way to use up remaining meat from the previous year's hunt to make room for an upcoming hunting season. For this particular recipe, I used a mix of elk and pronghorn, but most ground meat will work. Just make sure you account for variations in fat content. • *Yield:* 6 (1-pound) summer sausages | *Prep time:* 25 minutes, plus 5 days for salt curing | *Cook time:* 18 to 22 hours, plus 4 hours to bloom | *Grill/smoker:* electric smoker | *Chips:* alderwood

2 pounds ground beef or pork fat

5 pounds ground venison

3 tablespoon minced fresh garlic

1½ teaspoons curing salt

1 tablespoon freshly cracked black pepper

3 tablespoons brown sugar

1 tablespoon fennel seed

1 tablespoon dried basil

1 tablespoon liquid smoke

1 teaspoon onion powder

1 teaspoon mustard seed

1 teaspoon pure vanilla extract

½ teaspoon powdered thyme

½ teaspoon coriander seed

½ teaspoon celery seed

1. In a large bowl, mix together ground fat, ground meat, garlic, curing salt, cracked pepper, brown sugar, fennel seed, dried basil, liquid smoke, onion powder, mustard seed, vanilla extract, thyme, coriander seed, and celery seed.

2. Once well mixed, move the mixture to a 2-inch-deep roasting pan and pack firmly.

3. Cover the mixture and move to refrigerator.

4. Each day, turn, mix, and massage the meat mixture to ensure the curing salt is well incorporated.

5. After 3 or 4 days, pull the mixture from the refrigerator and divide into 6 even sections. Massage each well and form it into a tightly packed, oblong "loaf."

6. Lay out an 18-inch piece of plastic wrap and place your first "loaf" about 4 inches from the end of the piece of plastic wrap. Pull the wrap tightly and fold it over the meat. Roll the wrap tightly around the meat, smoothing and shaping as you go, until the sausage is evenly shaped as a tube. Twist the ends of the plastic wrap to seal.

7. Lay out a 10-inch piece of aluminum foil. Place the plastic-wrapped meat tube in the center of the foil and wrap tightly. Set aside.

8. Repeat steps 6 and 7 for each section of meat. Return the newly wrapped sausages to the refrigerator for another 24 hours.

9. Bring your smoker up to 150°F, and smoke your sausage inside of the foil wraps for 6 hours.

10. Carefully remove the foil and plastic wrap. They will be very hot and juices will have collected inside the wrapping. Pour those juices out, turn the smoker up to 160°F, and return the unwrapped sausages to the smoker.

11. After 10 hours have passed, turn the temperature up to 170°F and smoke for another 3 to 6 hours, checking the temperature of the sausages occasionally. When the internal temperature has reached 155°F, remove the sausages from the smoker.

12. At this point in the process, it is important to quickly cool the meat. Most people will put theirs in an ice bath with water but I find it important to infuse flavor every chance I get, so I prepare an ice bath with apple juice and use that to cool the meat. The decision is up to you.

13. Once the meat has cooled to 120°F, pull it from the ice bath and place it on a flour towel to let bloom for 4 hours, which will allow it to oxidize and create a vibrant and more flavorful sausage.

14. Store in the refrigerator for 1 week or freeze for up to 6 months.

WILD TURKEY AND WILD MUSHROOM SAUSAGE

Spring is such an exciting time for culinary enthusiasts. Baby greens sprout, asparagus spears shoot up along riverbanks, and fiddleheads, nettles, and mushrooms can be foraged along forest floors. For hunters, there is an additional element of excitement—spring gobblers. Wild turkey tends to be drier and tougher than its domesticated counterpart, so I like to poach in broth or cream sauce to keep those juices from seeping out. It's also brilliant when mixed with fat and stuffed into sausage casings, and pairs wonderfully with wild mushrooms such as shiitakes, chanterelles, and oysters. I recommend using morels for the dried mushrooms in this recipe.

Slice and serve alongside fresh cheese and specialty mustards for snacking. Cook them on a grill and throw them in a bun with your favorite toppings. Chop them and put them in pasta dishes. The sky's the limit with these flavorful sausages! • *Yield:* 16 (4-inch x 1-inch) sausages | *Prep time:* 1 hour, plus soaking time | *Cook time:* 2 hours 15 minutes | *Grill/smoker:* electric smoker | *Chips:* applewood

4 ounces dried wild mushrooms, rehydrated and chopped into ¼-inch pieces, liquid reserved

sausage casing, optional

1 pound duck fat or unsalted pork fat (pre-ground, optionally)

2 tablespoons olive oil, plus more as needed

8 ounces fresh wild mushrooms, chopped into ¼-inch pieces

1½ teaspoons sea salt, divided

3 pounds wild turkey (pre-ground, optionally)

3 tablespoons minced fresh garlic

2 tablespoons onion powder

2 tablespoons lemon juice

1 tablespoon dried basil

1 tablespoon chopped fresh oregano

1 tablespoon molasses

2 teaspoons dried parsley

2 teaspoons paprika

1½ teaspoons dried thyme

1 teaspoon crushed red pepper

1 teaspoon freshly cracked black pepper

1. Use the liquid from rehydrating the mushrooms to soak your sausage casings, if using, and let them sit for at least 2 hours or as long as overnight.

2. If you will be grinding your own meat, cut the fat into 1½-inch pieces and return it to the refrigerator.

3. In a medium cast-iron skillet, heat the olive oil over medium. Add the mushrooms and ½ teaspoon sea salt, and sauté until the mushrooms are moist and flavorful, but not rubbery, about 10 minutes.

4. Remove the mushrooms from the heat, place them in a container, and place them in the refrigerator or freezer to cool. You don't want warm mushrooms heating up your meat or fat while you are stuffing the casings, or the process will be much messier than it needs to be.

5. If you will be grinding your own meat and fat, run them through the meat grinder using the ¼-inch plate. Ensure the meat and fat are mixed together well. In a large bowl, mix the meat with the mushrooms, garlic, onion powder, lemon juice, dried basil, oregano, molasses, parsley, paprika, thyme, red pepper, black pepper, and remaining salt.

6. Optionally, pull a small amount of the mixture from the batch and form it into a small patty. Fry the patty on the stove to ensure the seasoning is to your liking, and adjust seasonings as needed.

7. Once all the ingredients are thoroughly blended, move the mixing bowl to the refrigerator. You should be working with very cold ingredients when stuffing the sausages.

8. Prepare your sausage stuffer. Lubricate the tube with a little bit of olive oil and begin feeding the casing onto the tube. Tie a knot at the end of the casing and use a knife, skewer, or needle to poke a small hole right behind the knot. Especially in the beginning of stuffing, air will be pushed through the tube and the hole you poke will prevent a ballooning effect.

9. Place a large sheet pan under the sausage stuffer to lay the sausage on as the casing is filled.

10. Pull your sausage mixture from the refrigerator. Begin loading it into your sausage stuffer and feeding it into the casing.

11. Once you have finished filling your sausage casing, choose the desired length for your sausage links and twist them off. Twist clockwise for one and counterclockwise for the next. This will ensure you are not untwisting the one sausage as you move on to the next.

12. Lay your sausages out to dry, leaving space in between each link to allow air to circulate. Place a fan on them while you prepare the smoker.

13. Bring your smoker up to the highest setting. Place your wood chips in the smoker and an inch of water in the steam pan.

14. Once you have a good amount of smoke in your smoker, dab any additional moisture off of the links with a paper towel, line the sausages on the grate, and set the temperature to 160°F. Smoke for 1 hour.

15. Bring the temperature up to 200°F and smoke for an additional hour.

16. Once the sausages have reached an internal temperature of 160°F, pull them from the smoker and spray them with warm water to quickly bring the temperature down.

17. Using a clean, shed-free cloth or paper towels, dry the sausages.

18. Once the links have completely cooled, package them using a vacuum sealer or freezer bags.

Pro Tip: Don't overwork your meat, and be sure to stuff your casings as quickly as possible so the sausages don't get too warm. The result of poorly handled product is a grainy sausage link. If this happens to you, all is not lost. The flavor and texture is still perfect for other dishes. Try removing the casing, mixing with a bit of soft cheese, and stuffing peppers or mushrooms for the grill.

HICKORY-SMOKED VENISON BREAKFAST SAUSAGE PATTIES

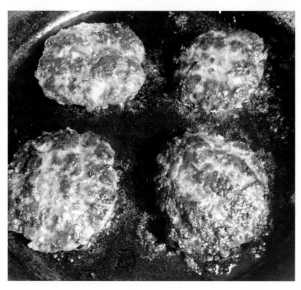

Don't you just hate it when you have to choose between bacon and sausage at breakfast? With the emergence of these sausage patties, the age-old breakfast conundrum has reached its demise. That's because this smoked venison breakfast sausage is chock-full of bacony goodness! • *Yield:* 8 to 10 servings | *Prep time:* 15 minutes plus overnight to chill | *Cook time:* 1 hour 20 minutes | *Grill/smoker:* electric or pellet | *Chips:* hickory

1¼ teaspoons ground sage

1 teaspoon paprika

1 teaspoon minced fresh garlic

½ teaspoon onion powder

¼ teaspoon allspice

¼ teaspoon ground nutmeg

¼ teaspoon sea salt

¼ teaspoon freshly cracked black pepper

⅛ teaspoon cayenne pepper

1 pound ground venison

½ pound bacon, diced

1 tablespoon pure maple syrup

1 tablespoon red wine vinegar

1. Mix all ingredients in a large bowl until thoroughly combined. Cover and refrigerate overnight.

2. Form the venison mixture into patties with a 2½-inch diameter.

3. Add wood chips or pellets to a smoker box and fill the steam pan with about an inch of water.

4. Heat the smoker to 225°F to get a good layer of smoke billowing in the smoker.

5. Position the sausage patties in rows on a parchment-lined grate in the smoker. Turn the heat down to 165°F.

6. After 1 hour and 15 minutes, remove the patties from the smoker.

7. If you are eating right away, heat a cast-iron skillet to medium and fry the patties for about 3 minutes per side.

8. To freeze for later, use a vacuum sealer or freezer bags. Separate layers of patties with parchment paper. Vacuum-sealing preserves the patties for 6 months; freezer bags preserve them for 3 months.

Game Meats to Use in Recipes

V = Venison (moose, caribou, elk, whitetail, and any member of the deer family)
P = Pronghorn (also known as antelope)
Be = Bear
Bi = Bison

Bo = Boar
R = Rabbit
WF = Water Fowl (goose and duck)
LF = Land Fowl (quail, turkey, and pheasant)
A = Alligator

Recipe	V	P	Be	Bi	Bo	R	WF	LF	A
Venison Steak and Avocado Tostadas, p. 22	✔	✔		✔	✔				
Montana Meatballs, p. 25	✔	✔	✔	✔	✔				
Hickory-Smoked Montana Meatballs, p. 26	✔	✔	✔	✔	✔				
Mozzarella-Stuffed Meatballs, p. 27	✔	✔	✔	✔	✔				
Red Pepper and Venison Stuffed Mushrooms, p. 29	✔	✔	✔	✔	✔				
Grilled Nacho Bites with Seasoned Antelope, p. 31	✔	✔		✔					
Buttermilk Steak Bites, p. 32	✔	✔		✔	✔	✔	✔	✔	✔
Wild Boar Salami Bites, p. 34	✔	✔	✔		✔	✔	✔		
Elk Caesar Salad, p. 36	✔	✔		✔	✔	✔			
Smoked Duck Salad with Goat Cheese and Pecans, p. 38						✔	✔	✔	
Spinach and Strawberry Salad with Crispy Duck Skin, p. 41							✔		
Asian Broccoli Salad with Pronghorn Steak, p. 42	✔	✔		✔	✔				
Smoked Duck Fried Rice, p. 45						✔	✔	✔	
Wild Smoked Onion Bombs, p. 46	✔	✔	✔	✔					
Grilled Steak and Potato Salad with Gorgonzola, p. 48	✔	✔		✔					
Smoky Maple Baked Beans with Venison, p. 51	✔	✔	✔	✔	✔				
The Perfect Venison Steak, p. 54	✔	✔		✔					
Smoked Mediterranean Venison Roulade, p. 60	✔	✔		✔					
Spinach-Artichoke Stuffed Elk Tenderloin, p. 62	✔	✔		✔					
Prosciutto and Fontina Stuffed Steak Rolls, p. 65	✔	✔		✔					
Burger Starter, p. 69	✔	✔	✔	✔	✔	✔	✔	✔	✔
Bacon Wrapped Venison Burgers, p. 71	✔	✔	✔	✔					
Blueberry and Brie Infused Bear Burgers, p. 73	✔	✔	✔	✔					
The Sequel to the Hunter Clogger, p. 75	✔	✔	✔	✔					
Tomato and Mozzarella Stuffed Bison Burgers p. 77	✔	✔	✔	✔					
Cheesesteak Elk Burgers, p. 79	✔	✔	✔	✔					
Venison Jalapeño Popper Burgers, p. 82	✔	✔	✔	✔					
Antelope Burger with a Portobello Bun, p. 84	✔	✔	✔	✔	✔	✔			

Recipe	V	P	Be	Bi	Bo	R	WF	LF	A
Goose Burgers with Fig and Bacon Jam, p. 86				✓		✓	✓		
Wild Turkey Burger with Swiss Cheese, p. 89				✓			✓	✓	
Enchilada Elk Burger with Green Chile–Corn Cake Bun, p. 90	✓	✓	✓	✓					
Coconut Milk–Soaked Bison Satay, p. 94	✓	✓		✓					
Cherry-Smoked Duck, p. 97							✓	✓	
Russian-Style Elk Shashlik, p. 99	✓	✓		✓	✓				
Honey-Soy Duck Skewers, p. 100	✓	✓	✓	✓	✓	✓	✓	✓	✓
Hawaiian-Style Boozy Boozy Duck, p. 101							✓	✓	
Smoked Cider Braised Quail, p. 103							✓		
Hickory-Smoked Maple Rabbit, 105						✓			
Cherry-Glazed Whole Smoked Pheasant, p. 107							✓	✓	
Bison Bulgogi, p. 109	✓	✓		✓	✓				✓
Grilled Bacon-Wrapped Meatloaf, p. 110	✓	✓	✓	✓					
Spaghetti with Montana Meatballs and Mushrooms, p. 112	✓	✓	✓	✓					
Chermoula Spiced Rabbit with Roasted Pepper Chutney, p. 114						✓			
Char-Grilled Venison Tacos with Mango Salsa, p. 116	✓	✓		✓	✓				
Old-Fashioned Jerky, p. 119	✓	✓	✓	✓	✓	✓	✓	✓	✓
Hickory Honey Jerky, p. 120	✓	✓	✓	✓	✓	✓	✓	✓	✓
Apple-Smoked Maple and Brown Sugar Jerky, p. 120	✓	✓	✓	✓	✓	✓	✓	✓	✓
Sweet and Spicy Jerky, p. 121	✓	✓	✓	✓	✓	✓	✓	✓	✓
Citrus-Thyme Jerky, p. 121	✓	✓	✓	✓	✓	✓	✓	✓	✓
Chipotle Mole Jerky, p. 122	✓	✓	✓	✓	✓	✓	✓	✓	✓
Green Chile–Cilantro with Lime Jerky, p. 122	✓	✓	✓	✓	✓	✓	✓	✓	✓
Sesame Soy Jerky, p. 123	✓	✓	✓	✓	✓	✓	✓	✓	✓
Whiskey and Spiced Cider Jerky, p. 123	✓	✓	✓	✓	✓	✓	✓	✓	✓
Bourbon Peach Jerky, p. 124	✓	✓	✓	✓	✓	✓	✓	✓	✓
Garlic, Cracked Pepper, and Sea Salt Jerky, p. 124	✓	✓	✓	✓	✓	✓	✓	✓	✓
Black Bear Pemmican with Dried Fruit and Nuts, p. 125	✓	✓	✓	✓	✓	✓	✓	✓	✓
Elk and Pronghorn Smoked Summer Sausage, p. 127	✓	✓	✓	✓					
Wild Turkey and Mushroom Sausage, p. 129								✓	
Hickory-Smoked Venison Breakfast Sausage Patties, p. 132	✓	✓	✓	✓	✓				

Acknowledgments

This book is a culmination of the practices I've learned from so many individuals throughout my life, and is a reflection of the inspiration, ingredients, and genuine love of creativity in the kitchen—especially when that kitchen is outdoors.

To my dear friends, family, and former coworkers who are willing to trade secrets, discuss ingredients for hours on end, and eat dinner incredibly late as I try to perfect recipes. Without them, the fun would be taken out of cooking.

To my parents and my sisters, who are always there for me and always have been. They inspired so many of the recipes in this book, with their varying taste preferences, dietary restrictions, and willingness to listen despite the distance that separates us.

To my husband, Chad, who manned the grill for many of these dishes as I shouted orders from the kitchen while whipping up sauces, typing up recipes, and styling plates for photos. Your continuous support and encouragement kept me afloat as I did a balancing act, juggling many projects at once to try to make my dream a reality.

To my sweet and saucy little girl, who at the age of one had a more refined palate than most adults and finds such joy in helping in the kitchen. Now, at the age of five, Coda, your willingness to try absolutely anything presented to you and your offers of "help" make me one proud mama! You are the sweetest piece of angel pie and my ultimate creation.

About the Author

© Austin Valley

Kindi Lantz discovered her love of cooking long before she could even reach the kitchen counters. Her grandmother gave her access to nearly every ingredient in the kitchen for her (mostly inedible) experiments. Kindi's culinary capabilities continued to grow even when she had reached her peak height at just under five feet. Her first job was as a chef's assistant on her relatives' farm at the age of 11. Throughout high school and college, she worked in a wide variety of restaurants—from American pub food to Japanese, Korean to Cajun, and down-home diners to Italian—and with each, she developed techniques and expanded her culinary expertise. For the better part of a decade, Kindi managed and even took on part ownership of a gourmet catering company in the Portland, Oregon, metro area. It was there, alongside some of the most talented chefs, planners, and entertainers, that Kindi's passion developed the most.

While in Oregon, something seemed to be missing from Kindi's own kitchen. Kindi was born and raised in Montana, and wild game frequented the family table. She often found herself craving deer, elk, and antelope. So when Kindi, her husband, and their young spitfire of a daughter moved back to Montana, they were thrilled to fill their freezer with wild game, and Kindi made it her mission to combine big-city culinary artistry with some of the finest-tasting and sustainably sourced meats in the world.

When Kindi isn't in the kitchen, she runs her own small business, FreeLantz, LLC, which provides digital marketing and SEO writing services to businesses that are looking to be found organically online. You can also find her tending to What The Cluck Farm, her small spread in Frenchtown, Montana, or spending time outdoors or crafting with her family.